こどもとおとなの
空間デザイン［対訳］

Designing Spaces for Children and Adults [Bilingual]

仲 綾子 ＋ TeamM 乃村工藝社

Ayako Naka + TeamM Produced by NOMURA Co., Ltd.

産学社

はじめに

　子連れで外出したときに、「こどもは楽しそうだったけど、わたしは
ちょっと疲れた」と感じたことがある人は多いだろう。一方で、こどもの
ほうが「大人は満足しているようだけど、わたしはつまらない」と感じた
こともあるだろう。どのようなところだったら、こどもも大人もともに心
地よく過ごせるのだろうか。その空間の特性を明らかにしたい。本書はこ
のような思いから生まれた。

　こどもも大人もともに心地よく過ごせるところとして、いくつか思い当
たる事例はある。しかし、これらを俯瞰し、共通する考え方や個別になさ
れている工夫などについて明らかにされたことは、いまだない。そこでわ
たしたちは、「こどもも大人もともに心地よく過ごせる空間には共通する
デザインの考え方がある」という仮説を立て、商業施設、文化施設、公共
施設、医療福祉施設などの設計者や運営者にインタビュー調査を行い、横
断的に検討を重ねた。

　本書は、この共通するデザインの考え方について論じるものである（第
1章）。その根拠となるインタビュー調査の内容は、写真とともに詳しく紹
介している。さらに、こどもが小さい時期に必要となる授乳やおむつ替え
ができるスペースについては、トピックスとして取り上げて総合的に検討
している（第2章）。併せて、こどもの空間を設計するうえで必要となる基
礎的知識として、安全性や身体のプロポーションなどについて解説してい
る（第3章）。

　なお、インタビュー調査でいただいた言葉のなかからとくに印象に残る
ものを008 〜 009ページにまとめて掲載した。その背景には、本書を単に

Introduction

When going out with a child, there are probably many parents who think, "My child seems to have had fun, but I'm a bit tired." Meanwhile, the child has probably thought, "The adults looks satisfied, but I'm bored." What type of space would be comfortable for both children and adults? We hope to uncover the characteristics of such a space. That is the sentiment behind this book.

When thinking of places that are comfortable for both children and adults, several examples come to mind. However, looking at these as a whole, there have not yet been any common concepts or individual solutions uncovered. Therefore, we hypothesized that "there are common concepts to designing spaces that are comfortable for both children and adults," and we interviewed the designers and operators of such places as commercial facilities, cultural facilities, public facilities, medical and welfare facilities, while performing a variety of lateral studies. This book discusses these common design concepts (Chapter 1) . It will introduce in detail the content of the interviews, alongside photographs, that support this hypothesis. Furthermore, we have focused on and comprehensively investigated the topic of spaces that provide the nursing and diaper-changing facilities needed for small children (Chapter 2) . Along with this, we also comment on safety, physical proportions, as well as other matters as basic knowledge required when designing spaces for children (Chapter 3) .

You will find a list of phrases from interview answers that left a particularly strong impression on pages 008 and 009. This is because we do not want this book to be simply a design manual for child-oriented facilities, but one that answers, on a more fundamental level, the question of how people perceive "children," "adults," and "the future." It was a somewhat challenging experiment, but we believed that it would be this deep insight that goes beyond surface knowledge which would be crucial to the design of spaces that are

こども向け施設の設計マニュアルとするのではなく、より根源的に「こども」、「大人」、「未来」をどのように捉えているのかという問いに答えるものにしたいという思いがある。やや気負った試みではあるが、表面的な知識にとどまらない深い洞察こそが、こどもも大人も心地よく過ごす空間のデザインにおいて重要と考えた。気になる言葉を見つけられたら、その言葉が掲載されているページをたどって読み進めていただきたい。

　本書の執筆は、東洋大学の仲綾子とTeamM乃村工藝社（松本麻里、井部玲子、西本彩）が協働して実施した調査にもとづき行った。わたしたちはみなデザインに関わる者であり、同時に子育て中の母親だ。デザインと子育てという2つの主軸を共有し、こども環境のデザインというテーマのもと、2015年より協働しはじめ、これまでに科学館における授乳室の調査研究、複合商業施設におけるこどものあそび場のデザインなどを行ってきた。本書はその延長上のひとつと位置づけられる。

　この本は、こども環境に関心がある設計者、施工者、管理運営者、行政関係者、学生などに有用な知見を提示することを目指している。同時に、子育て中の方々にも読み物として飽きずに楽しんでもらえるように写真やイラストレーションを用いながら、過度に専門的な用語を避けて日常の言葉で語るよう心がけた。本書で紹介する事例には、ぜひ親子で訪れてもらいたい。

　こどもも大人もともに心地よく過ごす空間のデザインに、本書がすこしでも貢献することを願っている。

仲　綾子

※本書に記載された肩書は、インタビュー調査実施当時のものです。

comfortable for both children and adults. If you find a phrase that you like, we hope that you will go to the page number listed beside that phrase and start reading there.

This book was published based on a joint study conducted by Ayako Naka of Toyo University and TeamM Produced by NOMURA Co., Ltd. (Mari Matsumoto, Reiko Ibe, and Aya Nishimoto) . We are all involved in design as well as being all mothers currently raising children. We began working together in 2015 with the two common cores of design and child-raising. Based on the theme of designing environments for children, we have thus far researched and studied nursing rooms in science museums, designed children's play areas in commercial complexes, and more. This book is positioned as an extension of that work.

With this book, we aim to present useful knowledge to designers, builders, operators and managers, government officials, students, and anyone else with an interest in environments for children. We also want people who are currently raising children to enjoy the book as reading material without losing interest, so we did our best to use photographs and illustrations, and to avoid excessively technical terms in favor of everyday language. We encourage children and parents to visit some of the examples introduced in the book.

It is our hope that this book will contribute as much as possible to the design of spaces that are comfortable for both children and adults.

Ayako Naka

※The titles of all interviewees are current as of the interview.

Contents

こどもの存在そのものが未来なんだよ Children themselves are the future. ·····pp.034-039／大人がこどもを連れて行きたくなる空間です a space where adults would want to bring their children. ·····pp.028-033／親子で思いっきりあそび、自分で発見する体験や達成感を味わってほしいです I want children and parents to play to their hearts' content and discover their own experiences and accomplishments. ·····pp.048-053／子連れで出かけたときに、腰を落ち着ける場をつくりたかったんです I wanted to create a place where adults could sit down and relax when they are out with their children. ·····pp.040-045／こどもの素朴な視点や心の動きや感覚にふれることが重要です It is important to gain children's straightforward perspectives, the changing of their emotions, and their sensibilities ·····pp.060-065／こどもたちはクリエイティブな存在である Children are creative beings. ·····pp.066-067／お子様にもやはりガラスのない客席で舞台の迫力を体験してほしい We ... want everyone, including children, to be able to experience the power of theater from the seats without glass. ·····pp.054-059／考え方が自由で選択肢も多い未来になってほしいですよね I want the future to have freedom of thought and lots of choices. ·····pp.046-047／保護者が集える居場所はお子さんの居場所より少ないのです Places ... where guardians can gather and feel welcome are less common than places for children. ·····pp.074-079／こどもも一人ひとり人格があり、違って

いるのですから Each child has his or her own personality and is different. ⋯⋯ pp.080-085／こどもたちに、ひとりじゃないよ、このアートを通じて理解し合える人たちがまわりにいるんだよって伝えたかった I wanted to convey to the ... children that you are not alone, you are surrounded by people with whom you can have a mutual understanding through this art. ⋯⋯pp.094-099／こどもにとってはささいなことでも大発見 For children, even the smallest thing is a big discovery. ⋯⋯pp.068-073／このような日常的な事故は医学の教科書には載っていません These everyday accidents are not found in medical textbooks. ⋯⋯pp.100-105／こどもは未来創造可能性がある Children have the potential to build the future. ⋯⋯pp.088-093／こどもが生まれてから、まわりに支えられている、地域に生かされていると感謝するようになった Ever since I had a baby, I started to feel grateful for the support from those around me and encouragement from the community. ⋯⋯pp.108-123／適当さ、いいかげんは良い加減って言いますしね 'Half-heartedness' is important. After all, the Japanese word for iikagen ('carefree') literally means 'just the right level.' ⋯⋯pp.086-087／こどもに専門家として関わっている保育士の社会的地位を向上したい We want to improve the social position of nursery school teachers involved with children as experts. ⋯⋯pp.106-107／事故を個人のせいにせず、いかに製品や空間の問題として扱えるかが重要です it is important to see to what extent we can treat accidents as problems with products and space, rather than blaming them on people. ⋯⋯pp.134-139

Chapter

1

こどもも大人も心地よい空間とは

How can a space be comfortable for both children and adults?

　親子でお出かけできる場所が増えている。商業施設などが子育て世代の集客を、また公共施設などが子育て世代へのサービスの向上を図ってきたためともいえるが、その背景には国による少子化対策への積極的な取り組み[1]がある。その結果、社会全体として子育てを支援する環境整備への関心が高まっている。これ自体はよろこばしい状況だ。ただ、親子で出かけたときに、こどもか大人が、または両方が、なんとなく居心地の悪い思いをすることは少なくない。

　なぜ、居心地の悪さを感じるのだろう。その構図を明らかにするため、親子でお出かけする場所を主な対象に着目して「こども向け」、「大人向け」に分類して検討しよう。表1に示すように、以下の4つに分類できる。

❶主にこども向け、大人は付き添いとして来る。
❷主に大人向け、こどもが付き合って来る場合もある。
❸こども向けでも、大人向けでもない。
　（こどもも大人も好んでいきたくはないが、用事があるので行かざるをえない）。
❹こども向けであり、大人向けでもある。

　❹以外では、こどもも大人もともに心地よく過ごすことが難しいという構図が見えてくる。しかし、こどもと大人ではニーズが異なるため、このような「こども向けであり、大人向けでもある」という状況はあまり多くないだろう[2]。ここで、世の中に目を向けてみよう。実は、❶に該当する領域のなかでも、親が行きたいと思うようなこども向けのあそび場がある。❷のなかでも、こどもが理解できるような展示空間をつくりだした、本来は大人向けの博物館がある。❸のなかでも、親子ともまた行きたくなるような病院がある。このような事例には共通するデザインの考え方があるという仮説を立て、その内容を追究するため、先進的な取り組みを行っている施設を対象にインタビュー調査を行った。調査方法は次節にて詳述するが、その前に以下の点を補足しておきたい。

　こどもも大人もともに心地よく過ごす空間、というと「子育ては限られた期間なのだから、どちらもすこし我慢してお互いに付き合えばいいのでは」という声が聞こえてくる。この問いに対しては、わたしたちが調査のなかでたびたび目にしたシーンをもって答えたい。本来、施設の主な対象がこども向け／大人向けに関わらず、そこでこどもも大人もともに心地よ

1. Redefining the nature of "children first"

The amount of places that children and parents can visit together is growing. While this could be attributed to the fact that commercial facilities are taking measures to draw in customers of the child-raising generation and that public facilities are striving to improve service for this generation, it is mainly caused by proactive efforts by the nation to counteract the declining birthrate[*1]. As a result, society as a whole is showing a growing interest in environmental improvements to support child-raising. This by itself is a wonderful thing. However, when a parent and child go out together, it is not uncommon for either or both to experience some form of discomfort.

What is the reason for this discomfort? In order to uncover its structure, let's categorize the places that children and parents visit together by focusing on whether they target mainly children or adults. As shown in Table 1, these can be divided into the following four categories.

❶ Mainly child-oriented; adults come along.
❷ Mainly adult-oriented; children sometimes come along.
❸ Neither child- nor adult-oriented.
(Neither children nor adults willingly go there, but it cannot be avoided.)

表1　主な対象 (こども／大人) による施設の分類
Table1 Facilities categorized by main target (children/adults)

		主な対象 Main Target		例
		こども Children	大人 Adults	Examples
❶	主にこども向け、大人は付き添い Mainly child-oriented; adults come along	◯	✕	・いくつかのテーマパーク※ ・おもちゃ屋 など ・Some theme parks ・Toy stores, etc.
❷	主に大人向け、こどもが付き合う Mainly adult-oriented; children come along	✕	◯	・美術館 ・コンサートホール など ・Art museums ・Concert halls, etc
❸	こども向けでも大人向けでもない Neither child- nor adult-oriented	✕	✕	・病院 ・役所 など ・Hospitals ・Government offices, etc.
❹	こども向けであり、大人向けでもある Both child- and adult-oriented	◯	◯	・公園 など ・Parks, etc

※ 例として挙げたなかには、もちろん大人も対象としているものもあるため、便宜的に「いくつかの」と表記した。以下の例はすべて同様の考え方で記載している。　Since the examples given naturally include some adult-oriented spaces as well, the term "some" was used for descriptive purposes. The following cases are all described using the same approach.

く過ごすことによって、単独の視点では得られなかったことをそれぞれが発見し、そして互いの経験を共有して笑顔があふれているシーンだ。これは、どちらかが我慢してもう一方に付き合う状況では、決して目にすることができない。わたしたちが目指すのは、このような空間だ。

たしかに、子育ては限られた期間だから、我慢してやり過ごすこともできるだろう。ただ、やり過ごし続けてしまうと、わたしたちが日々暮らす環境はいつまでたってもよくならない。また、この時期はこどもの今後の成長や家族の思い出に大きく影響を与える大切な期間だからこそ、ここで立ち止まって、こどもと大人がともに過ごす空間について考えたい。

この試みは、チルドレンファーストという言葉を安直に捉えがちな昨今の傾向に警鐘を鳴らすことになるだろう。チルドレンファーストはこどもを第一に考えるという姿勢を示しているが、ともすれば、この言葉を掲げながらも、本来の意味から遠く離れ、こどもに迎合するようなこどもだましとしか感じられないようなものに遭遇することがある。こどもと大人がともに心地よく過ごす空間について考えることは、こどもを第一に考えることと一見矛盾するように思われるかもしれないが、本質的にこどもにとってどのような空間が最も望ましいかを考えるという点で、根底でつながっているはずだ。

表2　**主な対象（こども／大人）と施設の用途分類の関係**
Table2　Relationship between main target（children/adults）and facility use categories

	❶ 主にこども向け 大人は付き添い Mainly child-oriented; adults come along	❷ 主に大人向け こどもが付き合う Mainly adult-oriented; children come along	❸ こども向けでも 大人向けでもない Neither child- nor adult-oriented
1.商業施設 Commercial facilities		事例／Case 1-1, 1-2, 1-3	
2.文化施設 Cultural facilities		事例／Case 2-1, 2-2, 2-3	
3.公共施設 Public facilities	事例／Case 3-1, 3-2, 3-3		
4.医療福祉施設 Medical and welfare facilities			事例／Case 4-1, 4-2, 4-3

❹ Both child- and adult-oriented.

Besides ❹, we can see that these are structured in such a way that makes it difficult for children and adults to have a pleasant time together. However, places like these that are "both child- and adult-oriented" [*2] are probably scarce due to the differing needs of children and adults. Now, let's shift our focus to the real world. Children's play areas in category ❶ that adults enjoy visiting do exist. There are adult-oriented museums in category ❷ that have begun to create exhibit spaces that children can understand. There are hospitals in category ❸ that both children and adults want to visit again. We hypothesized that such cases share common approaches to design, and, in order to closely examine these approaches, we conducted interviews at facilities that implement such forward-thinking efforts. The study method is described in the next section, but before that, let me add the following note.

When we speak of a "space that is comfortable for both children and adults," we sometimes hear the opinion, "Time spent raising children is limited, so children and adults should both have a bit of tolerance and socialize with one another." In response, let me share a scene that we encountered many times in our study. In this scene, smiles abound as both children and adults feel comfortable in the facility regardless of who the original target was. This leads them both to discover things neither would have noticed from their own perspective and to share their experiences with one another. This would not be possible if one simply tolerated the situation and went along with the other. This is the kind of space that we aim to create.

Of course, it is true that child-raising does only take up a limited amount of time, so it is possible for both parties to simple tolerate each other's activities. However, if we continue to spend time together under these circumstances, our daily environments will never improve. Furthermore, this is an important time that has a major influence on a child's future growth and family memories, so I would like to take a moment to consider a space in which both children and adults can spend time together.

This experiment will probably set off alarm bells for those caught up in the recent "children first" trend. "Children first" expresses the idea of considering our children before anything else, but these words have been stretched far beyond their original meaning, making some spaces feel as if they are simply pandering to children. You might think that considering spaces where children and adults can both be comfortable seems to contradict the idea of considering our children first. However, the concept is fundamentally linked to thinking about what kinds of spaces are most desirable for children.

2. 調査のフレーム

　インタビュー調査を行うにあたり、前述の主な利用対象（こども／大人）に着目して、❶❷❸の領域を網羅するよう対象施設を選定した。好事例を収集して整理すると、表2に示すように、これらの領域は施設の一般的な用途分類と重なることがわかったため、参照しやすさに配慮し、表3に示す商業施設、文化施設、公共施設、医療福祉施設の4カテゴリーで構成し直して記述することとした。調査対象施設は各カテゴリー3施設とし、さらに特筆すべき点がある施設を各カテゴリー1施設取り上げ、コラムと位置づけて記載した。また、とりわけ乳児期に必要なベビー休憩室については、トピックスとして詳述した。

　インタビュー調査は、主に施設の運営に携わっている方々に対して行ったが、プロジェクトのコンセプトやプロセスを理解することが必要となる

表3　掲載事例の分類
Table3 Categorization of Cases

カテゴリー Category		施設名　Name of facility
1. 商業施設 Commercial facilities	事例／Case 1-1	湘南 T-SITE　SHONAN T-SITE
	事例／Case 1-2	ハッピーローソン山下公園店　HAPPY LAWSON Yamashita-Koen Store
	事例／Case 1-3	タリーズコーヒー キッズコミュ グランツリー武蔵小杉店 Tully's Coffee Kids Commu GRAND TREE Musashikosugi Store
	Column1	ブラウンズフィールド　Brown's Field
2. 文化施設 Cultural facilities	事例／Case 2-1	国立科学博物館 親と子のたんけんひろば コンパス National Museum of Nature and Science ComPaSS Exploration Area for Families with Children
	事例／Case 2-2	劇団四季　Shiki Theatre Company
	事例／Case 2-3	Museum Start あいうえの　Museum Start i-Ueno
	Column2	ナショナル ギャラリー シンガポール　National Gallery Singapore
3. 公共施設 Public facilities	事例／Case 3-1	三鷹市星と森と絵本の家 Mitaka Picture Book House in the Astronomical Observatory Forest
	事例／Case 3-2	八王子市親子つどいの広場 ゆめきっず Hachioji City Playground for Children and Parents Yume Kids
	事例／Case 3-3	横浜市 青葉区地域子育て支援拠点 ラフール City of Yokohama Aoba Childcare Support Center Lafull
	Column3	岡さんのいえTOMO　Okasan's house TOMO
4. 医療福祉施設 Medical and welfare facilities	事例／Case 4-1	日本赤十字社医療センター 周産母子センター Japanese Red Cross Medical Center Perinatal/Pediatric Center
	事例／Case 4-2	国立成育医療研究センター 病院 National Center for Child Health and Development Hospital
	事例／Case 4-3	緑園こどもクリニック　Ryokuen Children's Clinic
	Column4	社会福祉法人あすみ福祉会 茶々保育園グループ Asumi Social Welfare Society Chacha Nursery School Group
Topics	1	商業施設のベビー休憩室 Nursing and diaper-changing spaces at commercial facilities
	2	旅客施設のベビー休憩室 Nursing and diaper-changing spaces at passenger terminal facilities

2. Framing the study

When conducting the interviews, we selected facilities that covered ❶, ❷, and ❸ of the categories mentioned above that divide spaces by target (children or adults). When we gathered and organized successful cases, we found that they overlapped with normal categories for facility use, as shown in Table 2. Therefore, to make it easier to reference, we decided to re-structure these based on the four categories used in Table 3: commercial facilities, cultural facilities, public facilities, and medical and welfare facilities. Three facilities from each category were included in the study, and one additional facility with special areas of mention was chosen from each category; these were placed in columns. Additionally, nursing and diaper-changing spaces, which are particularly necessary during the nursing period, are the main focus of Topics.

Our main interview subjects were those involved in the operation of the facilities, but when we needed to understand the concept and process of a project, we asked those involved in planning and design. The interview questions are shown in Table 4.

The details of each interview are introduced as good practices in Chapter 2, but in the next section, we would like to show the common approaches used to design spaces that are comfortable for both children and adults that we discovered when examining all of these cases as a whole.

表4　インタビューの質問項目
Table4　Interview questions

1. 企画について Project	企画の経緯　Circumstances behind the project
	企画の意図（最も大切にしていること）　Intent of the project (most important aspects)
	企画と運営の齟齬　Discrepancies between planning and operation
	企画意図を運営者や利用者に伝える工夫 Ideas for conveying the project's intent to operators and users
2. 運営について Operation	自慢できるところ　Parts to be proud of
	親子の利用の様子　State of use by children and parents
	利用者に言われてうれしかったこと　Positive feedback from users
	利用のされ方で、驚いたこと　Surprising ways it was used
3. ヴィジョンについて Vision	こどもとはどのような存在ですか　How do you perceive children?
	こども連れの「親」についてどう思いますか How do you feel about the parents who accompany children?
	どんな未来をつくりたいとお考えですか　What kind of future do you want to create?

場合には、計画や設計に関わった方々にもお話を伺った。インタビューで伺った項目を表4に示す。

　各インタビューの内容は第2章にてグッドプラクティスとして紹介するが、次節では、全事例を概観することによって見えてきた、こどもも大人もともに心地よく過ごせる空間に共通するデザインの考え方を示す。

3. こどもも大人も心地よい空間をデザインする7つの指針

　インタビュー調査を通してこどもも大人も心地よい空間をつくるためのデザインの考え方として、図1に示す7つの手がかりが見えてきた。

1. こどもも大人も主役

　こどもが主役で大人は見守り役、または大人が主役でこどもは付き添い、ではなく、それぞれを主役と捉える。各々の重みを等しくする必要はなく、また、常にこどもを最優先と考える必要もない。ときに大人に重きを置いて計画するほうがよい場合もある。なぜなら、大人が心地よいとそれがこどもに伝わり、ともにリラックスして過ごせるからだ。

　わたしたちの出発点は、こどもも大人も心地よい空間を探ることにあるので、「こどもも大人も主役」というと、トートロジーのように感じられるかもしれない。しかし、調査を行った全事例がこの考え方をもっていた。たとえば、横浜市青葉区地域子育て支援拠点ラフールでは、こどもはもちろん大人もほっとできる（p.080）。湘南 T-SITE では、こどもも大人も同じ空間でのびのびと過ごしている（p.028）。日本赤十字社医療センターの周産母子センターでは、赤ちゃんだけでなくお母さん、お父さん、さらにケアをしている看護師の心地よさを考えて計画されている（p.088）。グッドプラクティスは偶然生まれたのではなく、「こどもも大人も主役」と明確に意図した結果として生みだされていることを重く受けとめ、これをこどもも大人も心地よい空間をデザインする指針の核と位置づけたい。

2. こども環境の専門性

　こどもを取り巻く環境に関する専門的な知識や技術が求められる。誰もがみな昔はこどもだったので、それぞれ一家言あるだろう。子育て中の親や祖父母世代には主張がある方も多いはずだ。もちろんそれらは傾聴すべき貴重な意見だが、こども環境の専門性を軽視すべきではない。専門的な知見は、長年の科学的な探究と着実な実践にもとづくものであり、個人的

Through the interviews, we discovered the seven methods shown in Fig. 1 as approaches to designing spaces that are comfortable for both children and adults.

1. Put both children and adults in lead roles

Rather than the children taking the leading role and adults playing the role of their guardians, or adults being the stars and children being along for the ride, they both take on leading roles. Both do not have to have equal weight, and it is not necessary to give the child priority all of the time. There are some cases in which it is better to place more weight on the adult when planning. This is because when the adult is comfortable, it passes on to the child and allows both to relax.

Since our starting point is searching for a space that is comfortable for both children and adults, it may seem like we are saying exactly the same thing when we say "both children and adults play the lead." However, all of the cases that we studied used this approach. For example, at Aoba-ku Child Nursing Support Center Lafull in Yokohama, children can relax but so can adults (p.080) . At SHONAN T-SITE, both children and adults enjoy a liberated experience in the same space (p.028) . The Japanese Red Cross Medical Center Perinatal／Pediatric

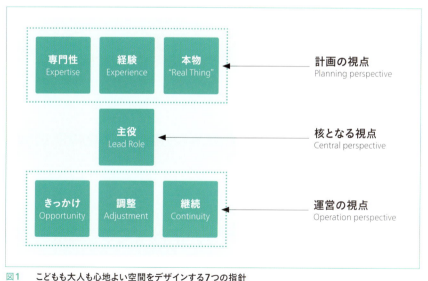

図1　こどもも大人も心地よい空間をデザインする7つの指針
Fig.1　Seven guidelines for designing spaces that are comfortable for both children and adults

な経験とは一線を画すものとして位置づけられるべきだ。

また、写真家の藤塚光政と環境建築家の仙田満が対談のなかで指摘しているように、文学でも写真でも建築でもこどもに関わることは、「なんとなく下に見られるところがある[※3]」。わたしたち自身も日々の活動のなかでそのように感じることが少なくない。しかし、専門的な知見をもって未来あることもの空間をつくっていると誇りをもって取り組みたい。同じような思いをもつ茶々保育園では、専門家としてこどもに関わっている保育士の社会的地位向上を目指している（p.106）。また、緑園こどもクリニックでは、院長が「子ども家庭省」のようなこどもの問題に特化した省庁について言及していることも、専門性を尊重する表れといえるだろう（p.100）。

3. 自分／他者の経験に学ぶ

経験には大きな力がある。上記の項目2で、専門的な知見は個人的な経験とは一線を画すと述べたが、一方で、個人的な経験には人を動かす力があるということも事実だ。たとえば、ハッピーローソンでは、ひとりのママ社員の経験にもとづくアイデアがプロジェクトの原点となった（p.034）。

ただし、ここで注意したいのは、自分の経験のみに重きを置きすぎないことだ。自分の経験が重要であるように、他者の経験にもまた大きな価値がある。それらに耳を傾け、もしかしたら自分の経験は偏っているかもしれない、あるいは他の多くの方にも似たような経験があるのかもしれないなどと俯瞰してみる姿勢が重要だ。JR東日本大宮支社では、駅にベビー休憩室を設置するにあたり、子育て中の社員が中心となってワーキンググループを立ち上げ、さらに駅利用者、駅員、運転士などの意見も収集した。これは他者の経験を尊重する好事例といえる（p.114）。

この姿勢を展開していくと、アンケートやインタビューなどの「調査」につながる。調査は、デザインとはかけ離れた小難しい学術的な方法ではない。デザインする際に、他者の経験に学び、また自分の経験の位置づけを理解するための有効な手段のひとつといえる。

4. 本物に触れる

本物に触れる機会をつくる。この言葉も多くのインタビューのなかで指摘されたキーワードのひとつだ。劇団四季は、「すべての観客に本物の舞台を」とモットーとし（p.054）、ナショナル ギャラリー シンガポールで

Center is designed with the comfort of not only babies but also mothers, fathers, and even care-giving nurses in mind (p.088) . It is important to realize that these good practices did not come about as a coincidence, but as a result of a clear intent to feature "both children and adults as the stars." This should be placed at the core of the guidelines to design spaces that are comfortable for both children and adults.

2. Recognize expertise in children's environments

Environments that surround children require expert knowledge and techniques. Since we were all children at one point, everyone has his or her own opinion. Many people have particular child-raising philosophies, from parents who are currently raising children to grandparents. While these are obviously important opinions that should be heard, we should not disregard expertise in children's environments. Expert knowledge is based on many years of scientific research and sound practice, and should be clearly differentiated from personal experience.

Furthermore, as photographer Mitsumasa Fujitsuka and environment architect Mitsuru Senda have pointed out in discussions, being involved with children through literature, photography, architecture, or anything else "has a tendency to be looked down on somewhat[※3]." It is not uncommon for us to feel that way during our own daily activities. However, we want to work with pride knowing that we are using expert knowledge to create spaces for these children with promising futures. Chacha Nursery feels the same way and aims to improve the social standing of childcare workers who are involved with children as experts (p.106) . In addition, the fact that the director of Ryokuen Children's Clinic references government ministries and agencies that specialize in children's issues, such as a "Ministry of Children and Family Development," can be considered a manifestation of respect for expertise (p.100) .

3. Learn from your own and others' experiences

Experience has a lot of power. In item 2 above, it was noted that expert knowledge should be clearly differentiated from personal experience; however, it is also true that personal experience has the power to move people. For example, at HAPPY LAWSON, an idea based on the experience of one employee who was a mother became the impetus for a project (p.034) .

However, it is important to remember not to place too much weight solely on one's own experiences. While our own experiences are important, there is also a lot of value in the experiences of others. It is important to listen to others' experiences and see the whole picture; we may find that we are biased toward our own experiences, or we may find that our experiences are similar to those

は、本物のアーティストの作品の横でこどもたちが自分の作品をつくることができる（p.066）。国立科学博物館の親と子のたんけんひろば コンパスでは、間近で剥製をみることができる（p.048）。ブラウンズフィールドでは、目の前の田んぼで育てた玄米や野菜を食事として提供している。これもこどもたちが本物に触れる機会といえるだろう（p.046）。

それだけではない。スタッフによる手づくりの展示品、プラスチックではなく木のおもちゃや床。これらも本物と捉えられる。つまり、ここで本物とは、専門家によるもの、最高峰の技によるもの、高価なものなどを指すのではなく、こどもに真摯に向き合ってつくられたもの、選ばれたものを指している。逆に、「こどもにはこの程度でよいだろう」という文字どおりこどもだましの姿勢で取り組んだものは、専門家の手によって膨大な費用をかけてつくられたものであっても、本物とはいえない。

5. きっかけをつくる

きっかけをつくりだすことに躊躇しない。よいことは自然発生的にはじまる、という素朴な期待に固執しない。はじめは意図的、あるいはやや強制的に機会を提供するようであっても、それをきっかけとして、こどもや大人が興味をもち、活動が広がることがある。

東京都美術館などによる Museum Start あいうえのは、美術館との出会いを応援するプロジェクトとしてはじまった（p.060）。また、岡さんのいえ TOMO で大学院生がこどもたちと交流している最初のきっかけは教授の半ば強制的な指示によるものだったという（p.086）。おせっかいを恐れずに、きっかけをつくりだそう。

6. 動かしながら調整する

最初から完璧にうまくいくことを目指さない。まずは一歩踏み出して、運営しながら調整し続ける。調整しながらすこしずつバージョンアップしていく。これはこどもの施設に限らず、どの施設にも適用できることだが、とくにこどもの場合は、予測できない反応や行動が多く、また、個人としては日々成長してゆき、集団全体としても社会状況に応じて変化してゆくため、物事を固定的に捉えるのではなく、臨機応変に対応してゆくことが求められる。

たとえば、三鷹市星と森と絵本の家では、来館者の反応をみながら展示内容に手を加えて、より伝わりやすいようにしている（p.068）。八王子市

of many other people. When JR East's Omiya Branch Office installed nursing and diaper-changing spaces in train stations, a working group was formed around employees who were currently raising children, and opinions were even gathered from station users, station staff, train drivers, etc. This can be considered a successful case of respecting the experiences of others (p.114) .

When this attitude continues to develop, it leads to interviews and other "studies." Studies are not complicated academic methods far removed from design. These studies can be considered an effective method to learn from the experiences of others and understand the position of our own experiences when engaging in design.

4. Experience the "real thing"

Creating opportunities to experience the "real thing". This is one of the common key phrases mentioned in interviews. Shiki Theatre Company's motto is to "provide all guests with a true theatre experience" (p.054) , and at National Gallery Singapore, children can create their own works of art next to those of real artists (p.066) . At the National Science Museum's ComPaSS Exploration Area for Families with Children, guests can see taxidermies up close (p.048) . Brown's Field offers meals featuring unmilled rice and vegetables grown in the fields that guests can see before their very eyes. This can be considered another example of an opportunity for children to experience the "real thing" (p.046) .

That is not all. There are exhibits that are hand-made by staff as well as toys and floors made of wood instead of plastic. These can also be considered the "real thing." In other words, the term "real thing" here does not mean things made by specialists, items created by the highest level of skill, high-priced items, etc., but rather things made and chosen sincerely for children. On the other hand, efforts implemented with an attitude that transparent ploys are "enough for children" cannot be considered the "real thing" even if they are made by experts for large amounts of money.

5. Create opportunities

Do not hesitate to create opportunities. Do not persist in the naive expectation that good things will happen naturally. Even if an opportunity is initially offered with a certain intent or somewhat forcibly, it may plant a seed of interest in children and adults, allowing the activity to expand.

Museum Start i-Ueno, a program implemented by art museums such as the Tokyo Metropolitan Art Museum, began as a project to support encounters with art museums (p.060) . Furthermore, at Okasan's house TOMO, the initial impetus for graduate students to interact with children came from half-obligatory instructions from their professor (p.086) . We should create

親子つどいの広場ゆめきっずの取り組みも、はじめからうまく軌道に乗っていたわけではない。市民の意見に耳を傾け、親子の様子を見守りながら、適宜調整して進めている（p.074）。

7. 継続するしくみをつくる

　企画や設計に携わった方々がデザインに込めた思いを、管理運営に関わる方々に伝えるしくみをつくる。時を経て、計画当初の状況を知る人がその場にいなくなったとしても、思いが受け継がれるようなしくみづくりが必要だ。よいデザインは語らずとも受け継がれてゆくという状況であれば理想的だが、現実的にはなかなかそうはいかない。

　たとえば、国立成育医療研究センター病院のホスピタルアートでは、作品を紹介するブックレットなどを活用している。また、オリエンテーションや研修の導入を示唆している（p.094）。継続するしくみづくりは、さらに、施設単体を越えて多くの類似施設に展開してゆくことも視野に入れたい。タリーズコーヒーでは、コミュニティーカフェ大賞を設け、よい取り組みの事例を共有している（p.040）。

　以上、こどもも大人も心地よい空間をデザインする7つの指針を示した。次章では、これらを導き出したインタビュー調査の具体的な内容を紹介する。わたしたちが感銘を受け、読者のみなさんと共有したい数々の言葉がそこにある。いずれの施設も、用途は多様だが、ここで示した7つの指針に触れている。

（仲 綾子）

※1　厚生労働省：少子化対策プラスワン、2002.9など｜Ministry of Health, Labour, and Welfare: Plus One Measures to Halt the Declining Birthrate, Sept. 2002, etc.

※2　たとえば、公園はこども向けであり、大人向けでもあるといえるだろう。本書で扱う対象は屋内施設としているため、ここでは論じないが、ある種の公園は、こども も大人もともに心地よく過ごす空間としてわたしたちが考える理想像のひとつだ。｜ For example, parks can be considered both child- and adult-oriented. Since this book deals with indoor facilities, we will not discuss this here, but some types of parks are an ideal picture of what we consider to be spaces that are comfortable for both children and adults.

※3　藤塚光政：富山県こどもみらい館、TOTO出版、1993　Fujitsuka, M. Toyama Children's Center, TOTO Publishing, 1993.

opportunities without worrying about being too officious.

6. Make adjustments as you go

Do not expect things to go perfectly from the very beginning. Start by taking the first step and continue to make adjustments as operations progress. Keep adjusting while making gradual upgrades. This can be applied not only to children's facilities, but to any facility. However, children's facilities in particular elicit many unpredictable actions and reactions, not to mention that they experience personal growth on a daily basis, and groups as a whole also continue to change based on the social situation. Therefore, nothing should be considered set in stone with such facilities; each situation must be handled as necessary.

For example, at Mitaka Picture Book House in the Astronomical Observatory Forest, exhibition contents are revised after seeing visitor reactions to make them easier to understand (p.068) . Hachioji City Playground for Children and Parents Yume Kids was not always on the right track either. They listened to the opinions of city residents and made appropriate adjustments while keeping watch over the children and parents (p.074) .

7. Create continuing schemes

Create schemes that convey to those involved in operation and management the sentiment that was put into design by those involved in planning and design. It is necessary to create schemes that will continue to be passed on even after those with knowledge of the early planning stages are no longer there. While it is ideal for good design to be passed down by tacit understanding, this is not easy to accomplish in reality.

For example, the National Center for Child Health and Development Hospital's hospital art utilizes tools such as booklets to introduce the pieces of artwork. In addition, the implementation of orientations and training is being suggested (p.094) . I hope that the creation of continuing schemes will expand into many similar facilities beyond a single facility. Tully's Coffee started the Community Cafe Award so that examples of successful endeavors can be shared (p.040) .

This concludes the seven guidelines for designing spaces that are comfortable for both children and adults. The next chapter will introduce the specific content of the interviews that led to these discoveries. There, you will find several phrases that inspired us that we wanted to share with our readers. While the applications vary, each facility touches on the seven guidelines introduced here.

(Ayako Naka)

Chapter
2

グッドプラクティスから学ぶ

Learning from good practices

事例1-1 こどもも大人ものびのび過ごす商業空間のあり方

湘南 T-SITE

　湘南 T-SITE は、Fujisawa サスティナブル・スマートタウン（Fujisawa SST）という、1000 世帯が暮らすまちづくりの一環として、2014 年にオープンした。店内は本屋を中心に、雑貨や飲食店など 30 のテナントショップが並ぶ。また、全体が BOOK&CAFE となっており、約 300 席の椅子やソファで、コーヒーを飲みながら本を読むことができる。

　建物は 1 ～ 3 号館があり、それぞれテーマ別にライフスタイルの提案をしている。1 号館は「趣味とデジタルライフの楽しみ方」、2 号館は「スローフード＆スローライフ」、3 号館は「親と子のコミュニケーション」。3 号館の企画を担当したカルチュア・コンビニエンス・クラブの尾花佳代さんは、出店の経緯をこう話す。

「この地域は、ショッピングモールなどの商業施設はすでに充実しています。そこで、必要なものを買うだけでなく、暮らしを豊かにするための施設が必要というまちの意図がありました。それが T-SITE のコンセプトに合致するということで、出店が決まりました。」

　そもそも T-SITE は、TSUTAYA の親会社であるカルチュア・コンビニエンス・クラ

マガジンストリート。ここから各コーナーへシームレスにつながる | Magazine Street. Each corner seamlessly connects from here

Case1-1 A look at commercial spaces in which both children and adults can relax

SHONAN T-SITE

SHONAN T-SITE opened in 2014 as part of a community-building project for a 1000-household community called Fujisawa Sustainable SmartTown（Fujisawa SST）. Inside, 30 shops, including general goods vendors and restaurants, line the halls centered around a bookstore. The whole area forms a "book & cafe" space with approximately 300 chairs and sofas where guests can read while drinking coffee.

The facility is composed of three buildings, each of which suggests a lifestyle with its own theme. Building I's theme is "how to enjoy hobbies and digital life," Building II's is "slow food and the slow life," and Building III's is "communication between children and parents." Kayo Obana of Culture Convenience Club, who was in charge of the planning of Building III, says the following of the circumstances of the store's foundation.

"This region is already filled with enough commercial facilities like shopping centers. Thus, the intent of the community project was the need for a facility where people could not only buy what they need, but also enrich their lives. That fit with the concept of T-SITE, so we decided to open this store."

ブが展開している複合商業施設。
湘南は「代官山 T-SITE」に続いて
2店目にあたる。どのような空間づ
くりを重視しているのか。

「T-SITE の空間づくりには大切に
している2つの軸があります。ひ
とつは本を中心としてその先にライ
フスタイルの提案があること。
もうひとつは家のような空間とい
うことです。フロアの中心にはマ
ガジンストリートと呼ばれる本の
コーナーがあり、そこからゆるや

児童書のコーナー。こどもの目線にディスプレイされている
Children's book corner. Books are displayed at children's eye level

かに周辺のテナントにつながっていて、私たちが提案するライフスタイルに沿った買い
物や体験ができるようになっています。また、家のような居心地のよい場所をつくるた
めにいろいろなものをそぎ落としたため、通常の商業施設に多くあるサインはほとんど
ありません。外からみたときに商業施設だと思えない、中にいる人が素敵にみえる、だ
から行きたくなる、そして居心地がいい。」

　通常大型の商業施設や公共施設では、案内上の利便性や利用者の注意喚起のためサイ
ンが多用される。しかも運営していくなかで新しいものが次々と足されていくため、結
果的にさまざまなデザインや色が氾濫する。それが居心地の悪さにもつながっている。
ここではヒューマンスケールの空間を重視し、すこしの不便には目をつぶることで過剰
なデザインの氾濫を避け、居心地のよさをつくり出している。

こどもをもつ大人のための、上質な空間

　もともとあった T-SITE のコンセプトのほかに、湘南という地域だからこそ意識した
点もある。

「ここは、結婚や子育てをきっかけに都心から引っ越してきたファミリー層が多く住ん
でいます。湘南 T-SITE では、そうしたファミリー層を一番のターゲットにしました。
いわゆる人気キャラクターがたくさんあるような施設をつくれば、こどもが喜ぶから大
人はついて行きます。しかしそういうお店づくりを得意としているところは他にありま
す。われわれが目指したのは、親が行きたいと思える店。大人がこどもを連れて行き
たくなる空間です。また、"大人が上質な時間を過ごせる場所"というのも意識しまし
た。ただでさえ子育て中の親は、自分がそこにいて素敵だなと思える空間に行く機会が
ありません。」

　店内を見渡すと、ベビーカーが通れるゆったりとした間取りのなか、ソファでコー
ヒーを飲む大人もいれば、絵本を読んでいるこどももいる。カフェの一画には畳席があ
り、お母さんと赤ちゃんがくつろいでいる。大人もこどもも、同じ空間でのびのび過ご
している姿が印象的だ。みな、買い物というよりは、居心地のよい空間を求めて訪れて

T-SITE began as a commercial complex developed by Culture Convenience Club, the parent company of Tsutaya. Shonan is its second location, preceded by the DAIKANYAMA T-SITE. What kind of spatial creation was regarded as important during its design?

"There were two core values that we considered important when creating space at T-SITE. One was that it would focus on books and suggest lifestyles based on that. The other was to make it a space that feels like home. In the center of the floor, there is a book corner called "Magazine Street" that loosely links all of the surrounding tenants so that guests can shop and have experiences that match the lifestyles that we suggest. Furthermore, since we chipped off a lot of different things in order to create a comfortable homey environment, there are almost none of the signs that you would normally see a lot of in a commercial facility. When seen from outside, you would not think it is a commercial facility. You think, 'The people inside look wonderful,' and it makes people want to come in. And it's comfortable."

Generally, in normal large-scale commercial facilities and public facilities, a lot of signs are used for informational convenience and to alert users. Furthermore, new things are always being added during operation, which results in an inundation of various designs and colors. This can lead to an unpleasant feeling. In this regard, the designers of SHONAN T-SITE created a comfortable space by placing importance on a human-scaled space and avoiding inundating it with excessive design by turning a blind eye to a bit of inconvenience.

3号館の外観。外には小さなあそび場もある　Building III's exterior. There is a small play area outside

A quality space for adults with children

In addition to the original T-SITE concept, certain aspects were brought to light thanks to the Shonan location.

"This region is home to a lot of families that moved here from central Tokyo due to getting married or having children. SHONAN T-SITE has made those types of families its number one target. We knew if we built a facility with lots of so-called popular characters, it would make children happy and adults would come along with them. However, there are other places that excel at creating that type of store. Our goal was to create a place where parents would want to come—a space where adults would want to bring their children. In addition, we also imagined 'a place where adults could spend quality time.' Parents who

3号館の外にあるこどもが大好き
なすべり台　Building III's exterior.
There is a small play area outside

いるようだ。

商業とコミュニティ醸成をミックスする

　湘南 T-SITE がさらに特徴的なの
が、コミュニティ機能も一緒になっ
ていることだ。とくに、こどもの英
会話教室や料理教室が入っている3号館では、地域住人に向けたイベントも頻繁に開
催している。

　「イベントの企画や運営は、コミュニティマネージメント会社と一緒に行っているもの
も多く、その会社のオフィスも施設内にあります。ここでは商業的なところと地域コ
ミュニティの醸成を、うまくミックスできないかと試行錯誤しています。」

　こうした商業施設がまちづくりの構想の一部となり、コミュニティスペースのような
機能を求められるケースは、今後増えていくだろうと尾花さんは予測している。

　実際、お客さんたちは湘南 T-SITE でどのように過ごしているのか。

　「コミュニティカフェでベビーマッサージのイベントを行っているのですが、イベント
が終わってからお客様が書店に来て、ベビーマッサージの本を手にとっていたりしま
す。隣接するカフェでお茶やランチをして、ママ友ができるといったこともあります。
書店を中心としたシームレスな空間の中で、人と人とのつながりができているのは、ス
タッフもうれしく思っています。」

　湘南 T-SITE はまちとともに生まれ、商業とコミュニティが自然と交じり合う新しい
商業施設のあり方だ。ここから発信しているライフスタイルが、この地域に根づいてい
くことになるだろう。「商業施設がまちづくりの構想の一部」となっている先進事例の
ひとつとして、将来コミュニティにどのような役割を果たしていくのか、今後も注目し
ていきたい。

（西本　彩）

are raising children usually don't have an opportunity to visit a space in which they, themselves, enjoy being."

Looking out over the interior, among the roomy layout which is wide enough for strollers, there are adults drinking coffee on the sofas and children reading picture books. In one section of the cafe, there is tatami seating where mothers and babies are relaxing together. The image of children and parents relaxing together in the same space is impressive. It seems that, rather than shopping, everyone comes here seeking a comfortable place.

Mixing commerce and community development

What makes SHONAN T-SITE even more unique is that it also serves as a community gathering place. In Building III in particular, which is home to a children's English conversation classroom and a cooking classroom, events are held frequently for community residents.

"The planning and operation of many of the events are conducted in collaboration with community management companies whose offices are also on the premises. This is a trial and error approach to see if we can successfully mix a commercial facility with community development."

Obana predicts that this type of commercial facility will become a part of the concept of community-building. She predicts that there will be more cases requiring a community space function in the future.

How do customers actually spend their time at SHONAN T-SITE?

"We hold baby massage events in the Community Cafe, and after each event, customers came to the bookstore and pick up books on baby massage. Some participants have also made friends with other mothers while having tea or lunch in the adjoining cafe. It makes the staff happy that people are making connections in the seamless space centered around the bookstore."

Created alongside a new community, SHONAN T-SITE is the new standard for a commercial facility where commerce and community combine naturally. The lifestyles originating here are sure to take root in the community. As a leading example of "a commercial facility that is a part of the concept of community-building," it will be interesting to see how it will fulfill its role in the community in the future.   (Aya Nishimoto)

▌概要 Summary
湘南 **T-SITE**　神奈川県藤沢市辻堂元町6-20-1
SHONAN T-SITE 6-20-1 Tsujido Motomachi, Fujisawa City, Kanagawa
http://real.tsite.jp/shonan/

事例1-2 進化し続ける子育て応援コンビニ

ハッピーローソン山下公園店

　ハッピーローソンは、ローソンの「未来のコンビニを考えよう」論文・アイデアコンテストで最優秀賞に選ばれたひとりのママ社員の「コンビニをママたちのコミュニケーションの場にする」というアイデアをもとにはじまった。ローソンのプロジェクトチームが企画を進め、2006年12月から半年ほど試験的に日本橋店を開店した。日本橋店の評判はとてもよく、常設店舗をという要望に応えて、2007年7月に山下公園店を設置して現在に至る。

　子育て家族を応援していくコンビニとして、ハッピーローソンにはベビーフードやおむつなどの販売、調乳用のお湯や授乳ケープの貸し出しなど、たくさんの工夫がみられる。これらの工夫に加え、空間づくりで目を引くのは、店舗に併設された休憩スペース「ハッピーひろば」にある大型遊具「キッズアイランド」だ。この遊具をデザインした環境建築家の仙田満さんにお話を伺った。

　「遊具で事故が起こりやすいのは滑り台とかブランコとか、こどもたちが自分で動きを制御できない場合だ。ここでは木のジャングルジムのような空間体験ができるようにした」と仙田さんはまず安全性に言及した。この大型遊具は高さがおよそ3mあり、こ

大型遊具「キッズアイランド」の
奥にカフェのカウンターがみえ
る ： A cafe counter can be seen
beyond the "Kid's Island" large play
structure ©環境デザイン研究所／
Environment Design Institute

Case1-2 An ever-evolving convenience store that supports child-raising

HAPPY LAWSON Yamashita-Koen Store

HAPPY LAWSON began with the idea of "making a convenience store a place for mothers to communicate." This idea was submitted by an employee, who was also a mother, to the "Future LAWSON 30th anniversary essay competition," and it won the grand prize. LAWSON's project team began planning and, in December 2006, the Nihonbashi Store was opened on a trial basis for about half a year. The Nihonbashi Store was received very well, and, in response to demands for a permanent store, the Yamashita-Koen Store was opened in July 2007.

HAPPY LAWSON has adopted many schemes in order to become a convenience store that supports families raising children, such as selling baby food, diapers, and other baby products, providing hot water for formula and lending nursing covers, and more. In addition to these schemes, a use of space that particularly draws the eye is "Kid's Island," the large play structure located in "Happy Hiroba," a rest space built within the store. I interviewed Mitsuru Senda, the environment architect that designed this play structure.

Senda began by speaking of safety. "The most common places for accidents to occur in

休憩スペース「ハッピーひろば」| "Happy Hiroba" rest area ©ローソン／LAWSON

ともは中に入って高いところまで登ることができる。そこから横に移動できるトンネルのようなところがあり、ぶらさがることができるネットもある。こどもたちは歓声を上げながら、この大型遊具の中をのびのびと文字どおり縦横に走り回っているが、これは、専門家としての仙田さんの長年の経験にもとづく安全性への配慮があってこそ、成立している風景だ。

親も子も、子連れ以外もそれぞれが楽しめるスペース

　一方、大型遊具のまわりをみると、ベンチに座ってこどもがあそぶ様子を見守って手を振るパパ、ママ、それに応えて手を振り返すこどもたちがいる。また、多くのパパ、ママは休憩スペースで食事をしたり、お茶を飲んだりしてくつろいでいる。休日にはビールなどを飲み、楽しんでいる様子もよくみられる。

　さらに着目すべきは、店舗とハッピーひろばをつなぐ細長いスペースに設けられたカウンター席だ。新聞を読みながらコーヒーを飲む老紳士やカップラーメンを食べる学生の姿などがみられる。子連れでも子連れでなくても、みんなが心地よく過ごせるスペースがある。「こどもの声に元気をもらう人とストレスを感じる人がいる。それぞれがうまくすみわけられるようにすることが大切だ」と仙田さんは教えてくれた。

play areas are the slides and the swings, or anywhere else that children cannot control their own movements. Here, I made it possible for children to experience space like they would in a wooden jungle gym." This large play structure is roughly 3 meters high, and children can go inside of it and climb up high. From there, there is a tunnel-like area in which children can move sideways, and a net from which they can hang. Children shout while running freely through this large play structure at literally every angle, a scene which is only made possible by the consideration for safety that comes from Senda's many years of experience as an expert.

A space that parents, children, and anyone else can enjoy

Meanwhile, when you look around the space surrounding the large play structure, you will see mothers and fathers sitting on benches, watching over and waving to their children as they play, and the children waving back at them. In addition, many mothers and fathers are relaxing in the rest area while eating or having tea. On holidays, it is also common to see them having a beer and enjoying themselves.

What merits further attention are the counter seats installed in the long, narrow space connecting the store to Happy Hiroba. Here, you will see older gentlemen drinking coffee while reading the newspaper, students eating cup noodles, etc. It is a space in which those with or without children can have a pleasant time. According to Senda, "Children's voices make some people happy and others stressed. It is important to keep these two apart."

Children themselves are the future

Finally, when asked how he felt about children, parents, and the future, Senda answered, "Children themselves are the future." Perhaps because this is something that

店舗の前には広場があり、その先には海が広がる In front of the store is a plaza, and beyond it lies the vast ocean ©環境デザイン研究所／Environment Design Institute)

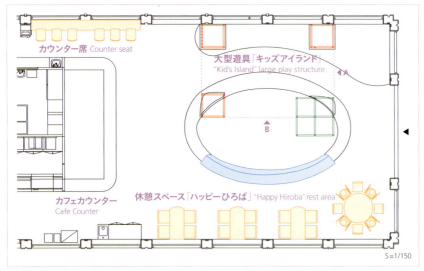

ハッピーローソン山下公園店平面図
HAPPY LAWSON Yamashita-Koen Store floor plan

© 環境デザイン研究所／ Environment Design Institute

こどもの存在そのものが未来

　最後に、こども、親、未来に対する考えを伺ったところ、仙田さんは「こどもの存在そのものが未来なんだよ」と答えてくれた。いつも考えていることなのだろう。この言葉が出てくるまでに一瞬の間もなかった。「こどもたちは将来に向かって育ち、われわれの未来をつくってくれる。20年後には彼らがすべての責任を負わないといけない。そういうこどもたちに元気にのびのびと育つ環境をプレゼントしたい。自分自身の未来のためにも。それにつきるよな」と、まるで少年のような屈託ない笑顔で語ってくれた。

　一方で、親に対しては「ぜひ、こどもにとってなにが大事かを考えてほしい。たとえばバギーは、こどもたちが自分の足で地面の上を歩くことによってなにかを発見する機会や運動する機会を奪っているのではないだろうか」と問いかける。たしかに、自分自身が親として振り返ると、車が多くて危ないから、一緒に歩くと時間がかかるから、こどもが寝てしまうと抱っこしないといけないからなどの理由で、バギーで出かけがちだったことに思い当たり、反省しかけたところ、「わたしたち建築家が、こどもと親が手をつないで安心して歩けるような空間をつくっていないことも問題なのだが」と仙田さんは言葉を継いだ。親を責めているのではない。ともに、こどもにとって何が大事なのかを考え、未来をつくりだそうという仙田さんの姿勢に学ぶことは、いまなお多い。

　なお、ハッピーローソン山下公園店は2017年7月にリニューアルオープンした。ひとりのママ社員のアイデアから生まれたプロジェクトは、子育て支援のコンセプトを貫きながら、現状に満足せず、さらなる高みを目指して進化し続けている。　　　　（仲　綾子）

立面図 A   1,500   2,040   900

立面図 B   900   3,000   1,500

S=1/150

大型遊具「キッズアイランド」立面図   © 環境デザイン研究所／ Environment Design Institute
"Kid's Island" Large play structure elevations

is always on his mind, these words came out of his mouth without a moment's pause. "Children grow up heading toward the future, creating the future for us. Twenty years from now, they will have to bear all of the responsibility. I want to give those children an environment in which they can grow happily and freely. For my own future as well. I will put all my effort into that," said Senda with a carefree smile almost like that of a small boy.

On the other hand, with regard to parents, he said, "I urge them to think about what is important for their children. For example, I think strollers take away the chance for children to walk on the ground with their own feet in order to discover things or get exercise." Indeed, when I reflect on my actions as a parent, I can think of many times I have taken my children out in strollers because I thought it would be dangerous with so many cars, it would take more time to walk together, or I would have to carry them if they fell asleep. When I began confessing this to Senda, he continued, "As architects, we are also at fault for not creating spaces where children and adults can walk hand-in-hand with peace of mind." He did not blame the parents. There is still a lot to learn from Senda's entreaty to create a future while considering, together with parents, what is important for our children.

HAPPY LAWSON Yamashita-Koen Store was renovated and reopened in July 2017. This project, born from the idea of one employee with children, continues to evolve and aim for even greater heights without being satisfied with the status quo while thoroughly carrying out the concept of child-raising support

(Ayako Naka)

┃ 概要 Summary

ハッピーローソン山下公園店 神奈川県横浜市中区山下町 279
HAPPY LAWSON Yamashita-Koen Store 279 Yamashita-cho, Naka-ku, Yokohama City, Kanagawa
http://www.lawson.co.jp/happylawson/shop/

事例1-3 地域の利用者に寄り添うカフェ空間

タリーズコーヒー キッズコミュ グランツリー武蔵小杉店

　2014年11月、神奈川県川崎市にオープンした複合商業施設グランツリー武蔵小杉の4階にタリーズコーヒー キッズコミュ グランツリー武蔵小杉店（以下キッズコミュ）はある。グランツリー武蔵小杉のイメージターゲットは、子育てにも仕事にも一生懸命な女性とその家族。キッズコミュでも、こどもと一緒のママ、家族向けの空間づくりを行っている。個人経営の店舗とは異なり、多店舗展開している大手コーヒーチェーンで、ママとキッズ向けの店舗を展開しているケースは珍しい。

　店舗デザインの大きな特徴は、店の中心に円形の本棚で囲われたキッズコーナーがあること。この本棚は背面のパネルがところどころ抜けていて、目線を遮らないように工夫されている。こどもはその中で、本棚の絵本を読んだり、そこにあるぬいぐるみであそんだりする。事業開発本部プロパティマネージャーの荒川和也さんは、デザインについてこう話す。

　「タリーズコーヒーのなかで、キッズゾーンを設けている店舗はこれまでにもありました。でも、従来の店舗空間の一画にキッズベンチ、テーブルを置く程度。ここまで全体をママとキッズに合わせた店舗デザインは初めてです。とはいえ、タリーズらしいデザ

ゾーンごとに高さや座り心地の違う席を設け幅広い客層に対応している | The store caters to a wide demographic with chairs of different heights and comfort levels arranged by zone

Case1-3 A cafe space that supports local users

Tully's Coffee Kids Commu GRAND TREE Musashikosugi Store

On the fourth floor of the GRAND TREE Musashikosugi commercial complex, which opened in Kawasaki City, Kanagawa in November 2014, is the Tully's Coffee Kids Commu GRAND TREE Musashikosugi Store (referred to below as "Kids Commu"). The target customers of GRAND TREE Musashikosugi Store are women who work hard in their careers and in raising their children as well as the families of these women. In this light, Kids Commu has created a space oriented for mothers with children and families. Unlike individually operated stores, it is rare for a large coffee chain with many stores to develop a store geared toward mothers and their children.

A major distinguishing trait of the store design is the Kid's Corner surrounded by bookshelves arranged to form a circle in the center of the store. These bookshelves are designed with back panels absent in some places so as not to block sight lines. Inside, children read the picture books that are on the shelves, play with the stuffed toys provided, and more. Kazuya Arakawa, property manager in the Business Development Division, speaks about the design.

"Before this, some Tully's Coffee stores had installed Kid's Zones. However, these

店の中心にある本棚で囲われたキッズコーナー。ここで読み聞かせイベントも定期的に行う｜Kid's Corner in the center of the store surrounded by bookshelves. Read-aloud events are held here regularly

インも残しています。こどもと一緒に過ごせる空間でありながら、お父さんやシニアの方、おひとりで来店される方も入りやすく、居心地よく過ごせるようにゾーニングし、店舗デザインも行っています。」

　たしかに店内は明るくやさしい色づかいで親子の入りやすい雰囲気をつくりだしながら、タリーズコーヒーの他の店舗と同じように木を基調とした落ち着いたインテリアを保っている。

子連れでくつろげるカフェづくり

　米国シアトル発祥のタリーズコーヒーは、2017年で日本上陸20周年を迎えた。上陸当初は銀座をはじめビジネス街に出店し、男性の利用が多かったという。

「徐々に駅ナカや郊外のファミリー向けショッピングセンターなど、女性が多い場所に出店するようになったので、それに合わせてメニューを増やしたり、店舗デザインを変えたりしてきました。ママとキッズ向けの店舗を展開するようになったのはここ2〜3年で、グランツリー武蔵小杉店がきっかけです。」

　同店はこどもと一緒のママの利用比率がとても高い。とくに平日の日中はバギー置き場にずらりとバギーが並ぶ。キッズスペースはこどもたちの触れあいの場にもなっており、一緒に本を読んだり、お絵かきしたり、ぬいぐるみであそんだりとほほえましい光景がみられる。

　メニューは、通常メニューのほかにママとこども向けのオリジナルが用意されている。カフェインレスのコーヒー、デカフェや、チョコレートで模様が描けるパンケーキ、キッズスープセットなどがそろえられ、親子でリピートする人もいる。

「カフェでコーヒーを飲みながら、こどもと一緒にゆっくりできる店ってそんなにないですよね。子連れで出かけたときに、腰を落ち着ける場をつくりたかったんです。」

Kid's Zones consisted of no more than placing kid's benches and tables in a section of the existing store space. This is the first store design that turns the whole space into a good fit for both mothers and kids. That being said, it still retains that unique Tully's design. While being a space where mothers can spend time with their children, it is also easy for fathers, seniors, and customers without children to enter the store. The zoning and store design are such that customers can be comfortable."

Indeed, the interior is bright with a gentle color scheme that creates an atmosphere that is easily accessible for children and parents, yet it retains the relaxed, wood-based interior of any other Tully's Coffee location.

Creating a cafe where parents can bring their children and relax

In 2017, Tully's Coffee—which originated in Seattle, Washington in the United States—marked 20 years since they first came to Japan. The first stores were opened in business districts such as Ginza and were mostly frequented by men.

"Gradually, as stores were opened in places frequented by women such as train stations and family-oriented shopping centers in the suburbs, changes were made such as adding menu items to cater to women and changing the store design. About two to three years ago, the company began opening stores geared toward mothers and their children, beginning with the GRAND TREE Musashikosugi store."

The store has a very high usage ratio of mothers with children. On weekdays during daytime hours, the stroller parking area is particularly full. The Kid's Space is also a place for children to interact, and one can see the joyful scenes of children reading books, drawing pictures, and playing with stuffed toys together.

In addition to the regular menu, the store offers original items geared toward mothers with children. There is caffeine-free coffee, decaf, pancakes on which kids can draw patterns with chocolate, kid's soup sets, and more, with some children and parents becoming frequent customers.

"There are not many cafes where adults can drink coffee while relaxing with their children. I wanted to create a place where they could sit down and relax when they are out with their children."

奥のソファ席は小さいこども連れでも気兼ねなくリラックスできると人気　The sofa seats in the back are popular for relaxing without hesitation, even with small children

店舗から自然発生的に生まれた取り組みが全国に広がる

　キッズコミュでは、定期的に絵本の読み聞かせ会も開催している。広報担当チーフ山口さほりさんに経緯をうかがった。

「もともとタリーズコーヒーは、地域のこどもに貢献することを目的に、絵本のコンテスト“タリーズピクチャーズブックアワード”を2003年から毎年開催しています。入賞作品は店舗で販売していて、キッズコミュの本棚にもこれまでの受賞作品が並んでいます。これらの絵本を活用する読み聞かせのイベントのアイデアが、店舗から自然発生的に生まれました。ただ、いつどの店舗からはじまったのかは、定かではないんです。」

　自然発生した読み聞かせのイベントは、現在わかっているだけでも、全国約100店舗で行われているという。広まったきっかけは、2012年に関東エリアにある店舗が、入店をためらいがちな子連れのママたちに気兼ねなく利用してもらえるようにとはじめた取り組みが社内コンテスト「コミュニティーカフェ大賞」で大賞を受賞したこと。

「このコンテストでは、全国の店舗が自発的に取り組んでいるサービスを発表します。タリーズコーヒーの経営理念のひとつに“地域社会に根ざしたコミュニティーカフェになる”があります。さまざまな立地があるなかで、お客様のことは店舗の従業員が一番知っている。だから、各店舗がお客様にとっていいと考えることはどんどんできる社風です。コミュニティーカフェ大賞は、その好例を共有する意味合いもあります。なかでも読み聞かせ会は、多くの店舗が取り入れました。」

　キッズコミュでは、ほかにも指あそびやパンケーキのお絵かき、クリスマスなど季節のイベントも開催しており、告知をすると予約が殺到するという。大手チェーンストアでありながら、地域の利用者に寄り添う各店舗のアイデアと裁量に任せる社風によって、地域に根ざしたコミュニティの場となっている。

　乳幼児を育てているママにとって、カフェでゆっくりおいしいコーヒーを楽しむのはハードルが高いことだ。だが、ここに来ればそれが叶う。こどもも大人も我慢することなく、おいしく、リラックスした時間を過ごせる場として、今後も多くの親子に笑顔をもたらしてくれることだろう。

（西本 彩）

イクスピアリ店での絵本読み聞かせイベントの様子 A picture book read-aloud event at the Ikspiari Store

An endeavor spontaneously started in a store expands nationwide

Kids Commu also holds regular picture book read-aloud events. I asked Public Relations Chief Sahori Yamaguchi about the history behind this.

"Since 2003, Tully's Coffee has held an annual picture book contest called the "Tully's Picture Book Award" for the purpose of contributing to children in the community. The winning books are sold in stores, and previous winners also fill the bookshelves at Kids Commu. The idea for an event in which these picture books are read aloud began spontaneously at a store. But we don't know which store started it or when."

This spontaneously started read-aloud event is known to now be held in at least 100 stores nationwide. It began to spread when a store in the Kanto area won the company's "Community Cafe Awards" in 2012 for an endeavor that it began in order to encourage mothers with children, who were usually reluctant to enter the store, to use it without hesitation.

"In this contest, stores nationwide present services that they offer voluntarily. One of Tully's Coffee's corporate philosophies is to "become a community cafe rooted in the regional society." Among the many locations that customers visit, the cafe employees know them the best. Therefore, the company's culture allows each store to quickly implement the services that they feel are best for their customers. The Community Cafe Awards also serve to share good examples of this. The read-aloud event was one of these ideas that many cafes implemented."

Kids Commu also offers other activities such as finger games, drawing on pancakes as well as Christmas and other seasonal events, all of which parents rush to reserve as soon after they are advertised. While Tully's is a large chain store, due to a culture that trusts the ideas and discretion of each store to support local users, it is also a locally-rooted community store.

For mothers raising infants, it is very difficult to relax and enjoy a delicious coffee at a cafe. However, that can be a reality at this store. As a place where children and adults alike can have a relaxing experience without having to be tolerant, this location is sure to keep bringing more smiles to the faces of children and parents   (Aya Nishimoto)

▌概要 Summary

タリーズコーヒー キッズコミュ グランツリー武蔵小杉店
神奈川県川崎市中原区新丸子東 3 丁目 1135 番地 1 号 グランツリー武蔵小杉 4F
Tully's Coffee Kids Commu GRAND TREE Musashikosugi Store
GRAND TREE Musashikosugi 4th floor, 3-1135-1 Shinmaruko higashi, Nakahara-ku, Kawasaki City, Kanagawa
https://www.tullys.co.jp/community/detail01.html

こどもも大人も解放される自由空間

ブラウンズフィールド

A free space that liberates both children and adults
Brown's Field

　千葉県いすみ市の豊かな自然の中にブラウンズフィールドはある。1999 年、写真家の
エバレット・ブラウンさんと料理研究家中島デコさんが、東京から引っ越してきたのが、
この場所のはじまりだ。2 人はオーガニックなお米や野菜を育て、自然の営みに即して循
環する持続可能な生活をつくりあげていった。やがて 2 人の生き方に共感した人が集ま
るようになり、敷地内にカフェがオープンする。

　カフェは中島さんたちの農や食、人とのつながりを大切にする思いが、そのまま形に
なっている。目の前には田んぼが広がり収穫した玄米が食事に出る。こどもは誰にとがめ
られることなく、土の上を走り回ってあそぶ。ショッピングセンターなどにあるあそび場
は、「走っちゃダメ」「登っちゃダメ」といった規制が多くなりがちだ。その点、ここは自
由そのもの。それでも、大人はおおらかに見守っている。「考え方が自由で選択肢も多い
未来になってほしいですよね」と中島さんは語る。

　ここにいると、寛容になれるのは、その環境と素材のよさを大切にする料理によって、
大人自身が解放されるからだろう。彼らは、この場所を訪れている時点で、「体によいも
のを食べ、ゆったり過ごす」という価値を選択している。その広がりが心やすらぐ故郷や
田舎のような場を生み出している。

　なぜ、それが可能なのか。ここでは、こどもを含めたお客さんの行動は、すべて「自己責
任」だ。スタッフは必要以上に干渉せず、それがかえって受け入れられている心地がする。
ここでの自己責任は、経営側の都合ではなく来た人に自由に過ごしてもらうためのものな
のだ。

（松本麻里）

ブラウンズフィールドにあるライステラスカフェの外観｜Exterior view of Rice Terrace Café at Brown's Field ©ブラウンズフィールド／Brown's Field

In the middle of the rich nature of Isumi City, Chiba is Brown's Field. This location was founded in 1999, when photographer Everett Brown and cooking specialist Deco Nakajima moved from Tokyo. Together, they began growing organic rice and vegetables and created a sustainable lifestyle on a natural cycle. Eventually, people who shared their lifestyle preferences began to come together, and a cafe was opened on the grounds.

The cafe gives form to the importance placed on Nakajima's and her team's farming and cooking as well as human connections. As the rice paddy stretches out before your eyes, harvested unmilled rice is served as part of the meal. Children run and play freely in the dirt without rebuke by anyone. Play areas in shopping centers and the like tend to have lots of rules like "no running" or "no climbing." This place, however, is completely free. Even so, the adults watch over their children in an easygoing manner. According to Nakajima, "I want the future to have freedom of thought and lots of choices."

Being here brings about a tolerance in visitors that is no doubt born from the feeling of self-liberation from cooking that values the goodness of this environment and its natural resources. By visiting this place, they have chosen the values of "eating healthy food and relaxing." The expansive grounds give way to a peaceful place that feels like a countryside hometown.

What makes this possible? Here, the actions of all guests, including children, are "at their own risk." The staff do not interfere more than necessary, and there is a comfort in knowing that one is accepted. The policy of self-responsibility here is not for the benefit of management, but so that visitors can spend their time as they wish.

(Mari Matsumoto)

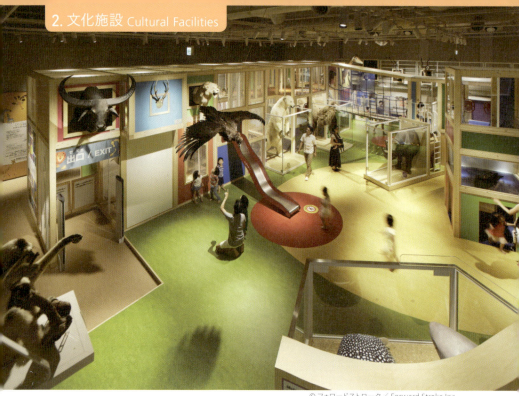

© フォワードストローク／ Forward Stroke Inc.

事例2-1 「なぜだろう?」のきっかけがあふれる学びの場

国立科学博物館 親と子のたんけんひろば コンパス

　国立科学博物館には、主に4〜6歳児とその保護者を対象にした親子のコミュニケーションを促す展示室がある。それが、親と子のたんけんひろば コンパス(以下、コンパス)だ。ここでは、動物の剥製をさまざまな角度からみることができる。フタコブラクダのお腹の下をくぐったり、クロサイの背中に乗った気分を味わったり。また、昆虫や植物を樹脂で固めた標本のキューブや自然科学系の本もたくさんある。自由にあそびながら、「なぜだろう?」と、こどもが知的好奇心を膨らませる仕掛けがそこかしこにある。開発を担当した神島智美さん、小川達也さん、渡邉百合子さんにお話を伺った。

　コンパスは、「親子のコミュニケーションを通じた未就学世代の科学リテラシー涵養」の入り口となることを目的として開発された。開発理由を、神島さんは次のように語る。「国立科学博物館では、展示や観察会、ワークショップはほぼ全て小学生以上を対象に行ってきました。ただ、未就学児も一定数来館していたため、こうした年齢のこどもたちが親と一緒に博物館体験をすることで、家庭にこの体験をもち帰れるように、親子を対象にした展示室を設けることにしたのです。」

自然科学系の本とちょっとした展示が混在している | Books on natural science and a small exhibit coexist

Case2-1 A place of learning where there are plenty of opportunities to ask "why?"

National Museum of Nature and Science ComPaSS Exploration Area for Families with Children

At the National Museum of Nature and Science, there is an exhibit room that encourages communication between children and parents, geared mainly at children between the ages of four and six and their guardians. This room is called the ComPaSS Exploration Area for Families with Children (referred to below as "ComPaSS") . Here, visitors can see animal taxidermies from a variety of angles. They can walk underneath the stomach of a Bactrian camel or experience the feeling of riding on the back of a black rhinoceros. In addition, there are many cubes containing insect and plant specimens solidified in resin as well as books about natural science. The exhibit is littered with devices to expand children's intellectual curiosity and make them ask "why?" as they play freely. I interviewed Satomi Kamijima, Tatsuya Ogawa, and Yuriko Watanabe, who were in charge of the exhibit's development.

ComPaSS was developed with the goal of being an entryway into "the cultivation of science literacy in the pre-school generation through communication between children and parents." Kamijima says the following of the reason for its development.

「本物」を通して、親子の コミュニケーションが広がる

コンパスの入室には整理券が必要で、安全のため時間制・入れ替え制になっている。利用の様子を神島さんが教えてくれた。

「各コーナーを自由に行き来し、それぞれの過ごし方をしています。間近でいろんな方向から動物などの標本資料をみることができるのが大きな特徴です。オープンから現在まで、当初の

自由に触ることができる、昆虫や植物の標本キューブ　Specimen cubes of insects and plants that can be touched freely

想定以上に多くの方に入室を希望していただいているため、運営方法については日々検討を重ねています。」

たしかに、土日にコンパスに入室するのは結構大変である。ただ、人数を制限していることで、ある程度ゆったりとこどもと向き合えるのも事実だ。ほかの展示室とはひと味違う明るい空間、楽しい雰囲気の中でお父さん・お母さんと一緒に「たんけん」することで、こどもたちには「科学＝楽しい」「博物館＝楽しい場所」とインプットされるようである。

コンパスの大きな構成要素のひとつに、ワークショップがある。「ワークショップで動物のお面を作ったのですが、動物園で撮った写真を使って家でも作ってみた、ということもがいて驚いたことがあります。また、ワークショップで観察した角や歯を、常設の展示室やほかの施設、家庭などでみてきたという声を聞くことも多く、ここでの体験がいろんなところにつながっていると感じます」と、主にワークショップを担当されている渡邉さん。ワークショップを通して、コンパスでのあそびや学びにとどまらない、親子のコミュニケーションの広がりが生まれている。この広がりをさまざまな場所で展開できるよう、ワークショップ集がまとめられ、活用に向けての動きもはじまっている。

こどもの成長に寄り添い、学びを深める

コンパスには多数の未就学児が来室するが、まだ小さいからダメ、という場面がない。ワークショップでは年齢別に道具を分けていて、たとえばハサミは、使いたいけれどまだ危ない、という年齢のこどもには小さいこども用のハサミが用意されている。高いところに上ったり、暗いところへ入ったりするのも、親の責任の下、OK である。危ないことを禁止するよりも、こどもの成長に寄り添って考える。そんな場づくりや運営の姿勢からも、コンパスが親子にとってより居心地のよい場所になっていることが感じられる。

"At the National Museum of Nature and Science, almost all of the exhibits, viewings, and workshops were aimed at elementary school students and up. However, because there were also a certain number of preschool children visiting the museum, we decided to design an exhibit room aimed at children and parents so that children of that age could experience a museum together with their parents and take that experience home with them."

Expanding parent-child communication through the "real thing"

Entry into ComPaSS requires a numbered ticket, and time and capacity are limited for safety reasons. Kamijima told me about how the room is used.

"Visitors go back and forth freely between each corner and each person spends time in different ways. A major feature is that guests can get an up-close view of specimens, such as those of animals, from various angles. Since opening, we have had many more requests to view the exhibit that we originally expected, and we reexamine how it is operated on a daily basis."

Indeed, it is quite difficult to get into ComPaSS on the weekend. However, the fact that capacity is restricted allows children to interact with the exhibit more leisurely. Unlike other exhibit rooms, this one lets children "explore" with their mothers and fathers in a bright, fun space, which helps children equate science with fun and think of museums as fun places.

上からも下からも観察できる
フタコブラクダ　A Bactrian
camel that can be viewed
from above and below

ワークショップスペース｜Workshop space ©フォワードストローク／Forward Stroke Inc.

　こどもたちの未来について思いを伺うと、まず小川さんが答えてくれた。

「コンパスでは、親がこどもとともに参加し活動することで、あそびからより深い学びにつなげることができます。親子で思いっきりあそび、自分で発見する体験や達成感を味わってほしいです。物事を偏見なくみること、いろんな目線でみることが大切だと思っています。」柔らかな口調の小川さんだが、そこにはこの空間に対する強い意志を感じた。神島さんもことばの端々にこどもたちへの強い思いをにじませながら、最後にこう話してくれた。「こどもたちにはこの空間を通じて、自然科学はもちろん音楽や芸術分野など、さまざまな方向に興味をもって羽ばたいてほしいです。」

　こどもの未来には、無限の可能性が広がる。科学には、「なぜだろう？」ということもの知的好奇心を引き出し、それを「生きる力」へつなげていく力がある。博物館として知識を提示することにとどまらない、「感じる力」や「考える力」を育む学びの場づくりが、コンパスを起点に広がる。

（井部玲子）

One of ComPaSS' largest components is workshops. According to Watanabe, who is mainly in charge of the workshops, "We made animal masks in a workshop, and I was surprised when one child said, 'We made another one at home using a photo we took at a zoo.' Also, children often say that they have seen the horns and teeth we show at workshops in the regular exhibit area, at other facilities, or at home, so we feel that the experience here connects to a lot of other areas." These workshops lead to expanded parent-child communication that does not end with playing and learning at ComPaSS. A campaign has begun to put together and utilize a group of workshops so that this expanded communication can be developed in various locations.

Supporting children's growth and deepening learning

A large number of preschool children visit ComPaSS, and there is nowhere that a child is too small to visit. At the workshops, tools are divided by age. For example, there are small, child-safe scissors for children who want to use scissors but for whom regular ones are too dangerous. It is even okay for them to climb onto high places or enter dark places under their parents' responsibility. Rather than forbidding dangerous things, a child's growth is considered first. Even from the perspective of spatial creation and management, ComPaSS gives the feeling of being a more comfortable place for children and parents.

When I asked the group's thoughts on children and the future, Ogawa was the first to answer.

"Since ComPaSS allows parents to participate and be active along with their children, play can lead to deeper learning. I want children and parents to play to their hearts' content and discover their own experiences and accomplishments. I think it is important to see things without prejudice and from various perspectives."

Ogawa's strong passion for this space was palpable even with his gentle tone. Kamijima also let all of her strong feelings toward children seep into her final words.

"I hope that this space will help children to become interested in not only natural science, but also music, the arts, and various other fields, and spread their wings."

The futures of children are full of endless possibilities. Science has the power to draw out children's intellectual curiosity and make them ask "why?" which connects to "a zest for life." The creation of learning spaces that foster the "ability to feel" and the "ability to think," not stopping with providing knowledge as museums, will expand with ComPass as a starting point.

(Reiko Ibe)

| 概要 Summary

国立科学博物館 親と子のたんけんひろば コンパス
東京都台東区上野公園 7-20
National Museum of Nature and Science ComPaSS Exploration Area for Families with Children
7-20 Ueno Park, Taito-ku, Tokyo

https://www.kahaku.go.jp/learning/compass/guide.php

事例2-2 こどもにも大人にも本物の舞台鑑賞を届けるしくみ
劇団四季

　1953年に創立した劇団四季は、日本国内に専用劇場をもち、ストレートプレイ（芝居）、オリジナルミュージカル、海外ミュージカル、家族を対象としたファミリーミュージカルなど幅広いレパートリーを日々上演している。

　お客様とともに「舞台の感動」と「喜び」を分かち合うという思いから、劇団四季ではすべてのお客様に舞台を楽しんでいただけるようさまざまな取り組みが行われている。その中で、こどもの観劇体験も大切にしており、日本全国のこどもたちに演劇の感動を届ける「こころの劇場」やファミリーミュージカルの上演を行っている。そんな劇団四季の専用劇場ならではの劇場設備の特徴や工夫について、日々劇場のサービスに携わり、クルー（スタッフ）の教育も行っている劇団四季・菅野達江さんにお話を伺った。

すべての観客に本物の舞台を

　全国の劇団四季専用劇場で展開している取り組みに、親子観劇室の設置と、こども用のシートクッションの貸し出しがある。この取り組みによって大人もこどもも分け隔てなく本物の舞台を楽しめる空間を実現している。

客席側から見た親子観劇室　The family viewing area seen from the seats

Case2-2 Schemes that deliver true theater experiences to both children and adults

Shiki Theatre Company

Founded in 1953, Shiki Theatre Company has exclusive theaters within Japan and stages a wide repertoire of street plays, original musicals, foreign musicals, and family musicals every day.

Out of a desire to share the "joy" and "inspiration of the stage" with their guests, a variety of efforts have been implemented to ensure that all guests can enjoy shows at Shiki Theatre Company. Among these are family musicals and "Theater of the Heart" performances, which provide children throughout Japan with the inspiration of theater, showing that the company places importance on the viewing experience of children. I asked Tatsue Sugano of Shiki Theatre Company, who is involved in daily theater services and also conducts crew (staff) education, about the features and devices of the theater facilities that are unique to Shiki theaters.

A true theater experience for all guests

The efforts developed at Shiki theaters nationwide include family viewing rooms and rental seat cushions for children. These have allowed the realization of a space in which

まず、親子観劇室について伺った。劇団四季専用劇場はすべて、客席後方に大人とこどもが一緒に観劇できるガラスで仕切られた親子観劇室が設置されている。室内には数組の親子が利用できるよう舞台のほうに向かって椅子が並んでいる。この観劇室はこどもだけのものではなく、またこどもを隔離する場所でもない。菅野さんはその位置づけを「いざというときのための場所」だと語る。

「私たちは、俳優が目の前で演じる舞台の臨場感を大人もこどもも分け隔てなく体験していただくことを大切にしています。舞台とお客様の間にガラス1枚があるか、ないかの違いですが、基本的にはお子様にもやはりガラスのない客席で舞台の迫力を体験してほしい。お子様が泣いてしまったり、じっとしていられなくなった時に一時的にご利用いただきお子様が落ち着いたらお席に戻れる場所があることが、こどもを連れた方の安心につながればと思っています。」

　親子観劇室は、子連れの親子が観劇するための場所というよりは、劇場全体を観劇に最適な環境とするための一時避難所的な（止まり木のような）存在であり、それが利用する親の不安を解消するのはもちろん、こどもの様子に気が散ってしまう他の観客への配慮にもなっている。

周囲の客席とも調和した、こども用シートクッション

　また、劇団四季では、こどもが舞台を観劇する際のサービスにも「観劇に最適な環境づくり」という視点が貫かれている。その代表的な例がシートクッションのサービスで、

四季劇場「夏」の客席後方にある親子観劇室　The family viewing area behind the regular seats at Shiki Theatre Natsu

children and adults can enjoy a true theater experience without being separated.

First, I asked about the family viewing rooms. All Shiki theaters are equipped with a glass-enclosed family viewing room located behind the regular seats where children and parents and children can watch shows together. The inside is lined with chairs facing the stage where several children and Parents can sit. This viewing room is not only for children, nor is it a place to isolate children. Sugano says that it is designed as "a place for when there is no other option."

"It is important to us that both children and adults, without being separated, are able to experience the closeness of the stage on which actors act before them. The only difference is whether or not there is one sheet of glass between the guests and the stage, and we generally want everyone, including children, to be able to experience the power of theater from the seats without glass. We hope that offering a place where, when their children start crying or won't be still, people can go temporarily until their children calm down, will lead to peace of mind for people who have brought children."

Rather than a place for parents with children to watch shows, the family viewing room is a temporary shelter (like a perch) that makes the entire theater an optimal environment to see shows. It eliminates the anxiety of parents that use it while also considering other guests who would be distracted by children.

Child seat cushions that match the surrounding seats

In addition, Shiki Theatre Company is also thorough from the perspective of "creating an optimal viewing environment" when considering its services for viewing shows with children. The best example of this is the company's seat cushion service, another area that considers not only the children that use them, but the surrounding guests as well.

The theaters regularly offer seat cushions for children whose height is 130 cm or shorter. There are a total of five cushion sizes—three thickness that are the same size as the regular seat surfaces, and two thicknesses that are half-sized. The theater crew members check the height of the child and position of the seat and combine cushions of different thicknesses. In this way, the device offers an easy viewing experience while considering the child's safety.

Even when the seat cushions are being used, the ease of viewing the show is maintained by keeping them lower than the eye-level of the guest sitting behind the child. In addition, the fact that children can sit all the way toward the back of their seat prevents their feet from kicking or pushing the back of the seat in front of them.

The crew members' consideration is also very thorough. Before the show begins, they eliminate the anxiety of watching the show with children and deliver peace of mind beforehand by informing parents of the location of the family viewing room and checking that children are comfortable with their seat cushions.

These considerations by the crew allow for a pleasant viewing experience. They allow both children and adults can be inspired by the same scenes together.

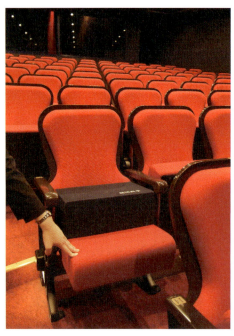

座席にシートクッションを置いた様子｜A seat arranged with seat cushions

ここでも利用することもだけでなく、周囲の観客への配慮がなされている。

劇場には、身長130cm以下の小さなこども用のシートクッションが常備されている。椅子の座面と同じサイズで厚みが違うクッションが3種、座面の半分のサイズのものが2種の合計5種類ある。劇場のクルーがこどもの身長や座席の位置などを確認し、厚みの違うクッションを組み合わせる。そうすることで、こどもの安全を考慮しながら舞台が観やすくなるよう工夫している。

シートクッションを使っても、こどもの後ろに座る観客の目線よりは低く舞台の観やすさは確保される。また、こどもが背もたれまで深く座ることができるため、こどもの足が前の座席の背もたれを蹴ったり押したりすることを防ぐことができる。

クルーたちの配慮も徹底している。開演前にはシートクッションの座り心地を確認したり、親子観劇室を案内しこどもと一緒の観劇への不安を事前に取り除き安心を届けている。

このようなクルーの配慮によって、快適に観劇ができる。大人もこどももみんなが一緒に同じシーンで感動を享受できるのだ。

実際の利用者の声を菅野さんに聞くと「親子観劇室があることが心の支え。こどもと一緒に来ることへの躊躇がなくなった」という感想も多いが「以前観劇した時は親子観劇室を利用したが、今日は最後まで客席で観ることができた」「数年前初めて観に来たときと今では、使うクッションの厚さが変わった」と語る人もいるという。来場者が劇場で心地よく過ごせたことが、演劇の感動に加え、こどもの成長を思い起こすきっかけのひとつにもなっていることが印象深い。

こどもの観劇体験を大切にする劇団四季の思いが安全や快適を目指した空間やサービスに反映され、観客に安心を届けるクルーに受け継がれている。これらの取り組みは、こどもだけを隔離することなく、そこにいる全ての観客が快適に本物の舞台を観劇できる空間づくりにつながっている。

（松本麻里）

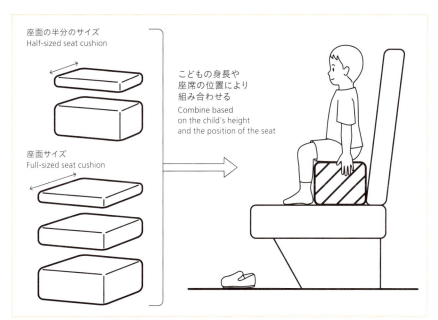

座面の半分のサイズ
Half-sized seat cushion

座面サイズ
Full-sized seat cushion

こどもの身長や
座席の位置により
組み合わせる
Combine based
on the child's height
and the position of the seat

図1　シートクッションの使用方法
Fig.1 How to use the seat cushions

According to Sugano, many actual users have said, "The existence of the family viewing room gives me peace of mind. I am no longer hesitant to come with my children." Other viewers said, "Although I used the family viewing room on my last visit, I was able to watch the show the whole way though in the regular seats today," and "The thickness of the cushions has changed since I first came several years ago." It is impressive how the ability of guests to have a comfortable viewing experience gives children an opportunity to experience the inspiration of the theater and to grow.

The value that Shiki Theatre Company places on children's viewing experiences is reflected in the spaces and services aimed at safety and comfort, and are handed on to the crew members who provide guests with peace of mind. These efforts have led to the creation of a space that does not isolate children, but allows all guests to have a true theater experience in comfort.

(Mari Matsumoto)

▌概要 Summary

四季株式会社 神奈川県横浜市青葉区あざみ野 1 丁目 24 番地 7
Shiki Theatre Company 1-24-7 Azamino, Aoba-ku, Yokohama City, Kanagawa
http://www.shiki.jp/

事例2-3 ミュージアムが連携し、新たな価値の交流をつくる
Museum Start あいうえの

Museum Start あいうえの（以下あいうえの）は、東京の上野公園に集まる美術館・博物館・動物園・図書館・音楽ホール・芸術大学など、9つの文化施設[1] が連携し、公園全体をフィールドに、こどもたちが各施設を行き交い、学び合えるプロジェクトとして2013年にスタートした。

プロジェクトには活動の柱としてファミリー向け・学校向けプログラムがあるが、児童養護施設のこどもや経済的に困難な状況にあることも、また在留外国人で文化的困難を抱えることもを対象とする「社会的包括」の目的をもつ活動もはじまっている。「社会的包括」とはすべての人びとを孤独や排除や摩擦から援護し、健康で文化的な生活の実現につなげるよう、社会の構成員として包み支え合うことだ。このような活動を実施している美術館は少なく、新しい試みで、あいうえのはさまざまなこどもたちがミュージアムと出会う入口となっている。

上野公園全体が有機的に連動するプログラム

あいうえのを担当する東京都美術館・学芸員の稲庭彩和子さんはプロジェクト立ち上

アートスタディルームでの、アート・コミュニケータのための基礎講座の様子 | Principal session for art communicators in the Art Study Room ©東京都美術館／Tokyo Metropolitan Art Museum

Case2-3 Museums cooperating to form a new exchange

Museum Start i-Ueno

Museum Start i-Ueno (referred to below as "i-Ueno") is a project that began in 2013 that allows children to visit various cultural facilities in Ueno Park and learn from each one, covering the entire park. It is a collaboration between nine facilities[1], consisting of museums, a zoo, a library, a music hall, and an art university.

In addition to the programs for families and schools that serve as the central pillar of the activities, a social inclusion program has also been started for children in orphanages and those in difficult financial situations as well as immigrant children and youth facing cultural difficulties. Social inclusion means protecting all groups of people from isolation, exclusion, and social friction as well as welcoming and supporting them as members of society so that they are able to lead healthy and cultural lives. As there are not many art museums that offer these kinds of activities, it is a new experiment. i-Ueno is an entryway for a variety of children to encounter museums.

A program in which the entirety of Ueno Park works together organically

Sawako Inaniwa, the curator at Tokyo Metropolitan Art Museum in charge of i-Ueno,

げの経緯をこう語る。

「2012年から東京都美術館では『とびらプロジェクト』という美術館と大学と市民が協働するプロジェクトがはじまっていました。そしてこれからの時代には大人だけでなくこどもとも協働できるミュージアムを資源とした活動が必要だと思い、イギリス発祥の『ブックスタート』というこどもの読書を推奨する制度を参照して考えました。ミュージアムとの出会いも、『スタート＝はじめて・はじまり』をいかによい形、よい経験とするかが重要です。あいうえのをきっかけに、こどもたちがミュージアムを自発的に使いこなせるようになるしくみを考えました。」

　ここでツールとして活用されているのが、ミュージアム・スタート・パックだ。9つの施設情報が一冊にまとまった冊子「ビビハドトカダブック」とミュージアムでの発見を記録できる「冒険ノート」とバッグのセットで、バッグの表面には9つの施設のバッジがつけられる。

「作品を見て発見したことをノートに書きオリジナルバッジを集めてゆくとミュージアムでの自分の足跡が見える形になりモチベーションが上がり継続しやすいことが特徴です」と稲庭さんは教えてくれた。このツールのおかげで、こどもたちは自発的に楽しみながら物の見方を深めてゆく。

　9つの組織が連携するプロジェクトは、どのように実施されているのだろうか。

「このプロジェクトは東京藝術大学と当館が共同で運営事務局を担い、さらに7つの文化施設と連携しています。そこで一番重要なのは担当者同士が知り合い、信頼関係を築き各館のコンテンツが良い響きあいをするようになることです。たとえば、東京都美術館でゴッホが愛した作品を見た後に、東京国立博物館へ創作の源になった浮世絵を見に行く、というものもあれば、科学博物館で絵具の元となる鉱石を観察した後、東京藝術大学で石を粉にして絵具を実際に作ってみるというような企画を実施しています。」

　プログラムの特徴は、物をじっくりと観察すること。知識を先に伝えるのではなく、まずは対象となる物をよく見ることからはじめる。そして、「大人も、既存の知識や常識にとらわれないこどもの素朴な視点や心の動きや感覚にふれることが重要です。一緒に展示物を鑑賞しながらお互いの発見や感じたことを伝え合うと、自然と会話がはずみます」と稲庭さんは指摘する。大人もこども同じものを見て感じたことを共有するこのような対話を通して自分ひとりで見ていたときには気づかなかったことが見え、新たなものの見方の発見がある。

展示室（国立西洋美術館常設展）にてプログラムに参加するこどもたちとアート・コミュニケータ
Children and art communicators participating in a program in an exhibition room (Permanent Collection, The National Museum of Western Art) ©東京都美術館／Tokyo Metropolitan Art Museum

左：ミュージアム・スタート・パック（2017年度版）／右：こどもが書いた冒険ノート　Left: Museum Starter Pack (2017 edition)／Right: Adventure notes written by a child ©東京都美術館／Tokyo Metropolitan Art Museum

speaks of the circumstances of starting the project as follows.

"In 2012, a museum, university, and residents had worked together to start a project titled the 'Tobira Project,' I thought that going forward, there would be a need for activities that would utilize museums where not only adults, but also children can come and work together. I was inspired by Bookstart, a system developed in the UK that promotes reading by children. I wanted to create a scheme that supported encounters for children with museums, using the museum-filled Ueno Park as a stage. When dealing with encounters with museums, it was also important to see how great a shape, how great an experience we could turn a 'start' into." I thought up a system that would allow children to make use of the museum of their own accord."

For this, the Museum Starter Pack is used as a tool. This is a set containing a "Bibihadoto kada Book"—a notebook that provides information on the nine facilities—an "Adventure Notebook" in which children can record what they discovered in the museum, and a bag, on the back of which children can collect badges from all nine facilities.

According to Inaniwa, "Children write in their notebooks what they discovered from looking at the art and collect original badges, which allows them to see their 'footsteps' and what they have accomplished, increasing their motivation and making it easier for children to continue taking part in the activities." Thanks to this tool, children deepen the way they see things while enjoying the experience of their own accord.

How did you accomplish a project in which nine organizations come together and collaborate?

"Tokyo University of the Arts and this museum jointly serve as the administrative office for this project while additionally collaborating with seven other cultural facilities. The most important point is that the people in charge get to know each other and build up a trusting relationship with one another so that the content provided by each facility work in harmony. For example, the program includes proposed itineraries such as first seeing the works that were loved by Van Gogh at the Tokyo Metropolitan Art Museum, followed by viewing the woodblock prints that inspired him at the Tokyo National Museum, or first seeing the minerals that are used to make paint at The National

アートスタディルームでのワークショップの様子　A workshop in the Art Study Room ©東京都美術館／Tokyo Metropolitan Art Museum

ミュージアム・スタートの小さな拠点「アートスタディルーム」

　公園全体をフィールドとして捉え、ミュージアム同士が連携する活動は、学芸員、大学の教員、プロジェクトに参画する市民など、さまざまな人びとによって支えられている。その活動拠点のひとつとなっているのが、東京都美術館内の一室「アートスタディルーム」だ。

　ここはあいうえののプログラムの実施会場として使われることはもちろん、プロジェクトに関わるアート・コミュニケータ※2のための講座、企画ミーティングなど、多岐にわたる活動の場となっている。そして、ミュージアム・デビューをするこどもたちにとって、ここはミュージアムと出会うスタート地点でもある。そこに置かれた家具、書籍、道具の数々は全てさまざまなプログラムを推進するために厳選されている。たとえば、テーブルはワークショップやディスカッションなどの用途に応じて高さを変えられる特注品だ。また、椅子は積み重ねられるので、広いスペースが必要なときには容易に場所を確保できる。アートスタディルームは小さいながらもプログラムの拠点となる空間だ。

　プロジェクトがはじまって5年が経った今、稲庭さんに今後への思いを伺った。「クリエイティブな活動を通じて次世代にミュージアムを継承していくには、さらなる工夫が必要で、その方法を模索しています。」

　これまであまりミュージアムを訪れる機会がなかったこどもたちをはじめ、誰もがアートや文化財などに出会うための「しくみづくり」をスタートさせたあいうえの。稲庭さんの言葉から、そのしくみをより深化させるステップに進みつつあることが伺える。ミュージアムという場の可能性は広がりつづける。その模索の最先端だ。

（松本麻里）

※1　9つの文化施設：上野の森美術館、恩賜上野動物園、国立科学博物館、国立国会図書館国際子ども図書館、国立西洋美術館、東京藝術大学、東京国立博物館、東京都美術館、東京文化会館（五十音順）　The nine cultural facilities are: The Ueno Royal Museum, Ueno Zoological Gardens, The National Museum of Nature and Science, International Library of Children's Literature, The National Museum of Western Art, Tokyo University of the Arts, Tokyo National Museum, Tokyo Metropolitan Art Museum, and Tokyo Bunka Kaikan

※2　アート・コミュニケータ：アートを介して人と人とをつなげていく人びと。従来の美術館のボランティアではなく、学芸員や大学の教員などの専門家とともに活動する能動的なプレイヤー　Art communicators are individuals who connect people with other people through art. They are not conventional art museum volunteers, but active players who work with experts such as curators and university faculty

Museum Of Nature and Science and then going to the Tokyo University of the Arts to actually crush the stones to make paint."

A distinguishing feature of the program is the idea of viewing things leisurely. Rather than conveying the knowledge beforehand, it starts by taking a good look at the relevant items. Inaniwa also points out that, "It is important to gain children's straightforward perspectives, the changing of their emotions, and their sensibilities before they are blemished with existing knowledge or common sense. If we convey to each other what we discovered and felt while viewing the exhibits together, it will naturally stimulate conversation." Children and adults sharing what they feel when looking at the same thing; this kind of discussion allows parents and children to see things that they did not realize when viewing it by themselves and allows them to discover new ways to see things.

The "Art Study Room," Museum Start's small center

The collaborative activities that use the entire park as a field are supported by a variety of people, including curators, university faculty, and city residents who participate in the project. One center for these activities is the "Art Study Room," a room at the Tokyo Metropolitan Art Museum.

In addition to being a place to conduct programs, it also used for a wide range of activities, such as courses for art communicators[2] involved in the project and planning meetings. For children making their museum debut, it is also a starting point for encountering museums. Each piece of furniture, book, and tool in the room is specifically chosen to promote a variety of programs. For example, the tables are custom-made and can change height based on whether they will be used for a workshop, a discussion, etc. In addition, the seats can be stacked easily to ensure space when needed. While it is small, the Art Study Room forms the center of the program.

Now, five years after starting the project, I asked Inaniwa about her feelings for the future.

"I think that passing this museum on to the next generation through these creative activities will require even more unique ideas and so I am looking into ways of doing this."

i-Ueno is a project that started the "creation of schemes" to allow everyone—including children who have not had many opportunities to visit museums before—to encounter art and cultural assets. From Inaniwa's words, I can tell that she is moving forward with steps to further deepen these schemes. The possibilities of museums will continue to expand. They lie at the end of her search.

(Mari Matsumoto)

┃ 概要 Summary

Museum Start あいうえの
Museum Start あいうえの 運営チーム（東京都美術館 × 東京藝術大学）
〒 110-0007 東京都台東区上野公園 8-36
Museum Start i-Ueno
Museum Start i-Ueno Management Team（Tokyo Metropolitan Art Museum & Tokyo University of the Arts)
8-36 Ueno Ko-en, Taito-ku, Tokyo, 110-0007

http://museum-start.jp/

こどもも大人も自由に制作できる ワークショップスペース

ナショナル ギャラリー シンガポール

A workshop space where both children and adults can create art freely

National Gallery Singapore

　ここでは、2015年にオープンしたナショナル ギャラリー シンガポールに設けられた チルドレンズミュージアム内のワークショップスペースを紹介したい。このスペースは、「アートを通して未来をつくる」というコンセプトのもと、アクセスしやすいエントランスのすぐ脇に設けられている。こどもたちはここで自分の作品を制作できるのだ。こどもたちだけではない。こどもを連れてくるという役割になりがちな大人たちも楽しそうに制作している。ここでの主役はこどもであり、大人でもある。ワークショップスペースは毎年更新されているが、こどもも大人もいつも自由に作品を制作できることに変わりはない。

　ナショナル ギャラリー シンガポールは、かつて最高裁判所と市庁舎として使用されていた歴史的建造物のリノベーションであり、外観は重厚感があるが、不思議と権威的な雰囲気はない。その理由のひとつとして、このようなこどものためのスペースがギャラリーの真ん中に配置されていることが挙げられる。

　ディレクターのイェ・シュファンさんによると、「こどもたちはクリエィティブな存在である」という認識を前提としたうえで、このようなこどもたちを支える「多様で（diverse）包括的な（inclusive）未来」を目指しているという。これらは日本でもよく耳にするキーワードであり、共通する普遍的な傾向といえる。　　　　　　　（仲 綾子）

正面の壁にアーティストの作品が設置されている　Works of art by artists are displayed on the front wall

Here, I would like to introduce the workshop space in the Children's Museum at National Gallery Singapore, which opened in 2015. This space was built right next to the easily accessible entrance based on the concept of "shaping our future through art." Children can create their own works of art in this space. And it's not just children. Adults, who tend to play the role of accompanying the children, also enjoy creating art. Here, both children and adults take a leading role. Although the Children's Museum is updated every year, children and adults are always free to create works of art in the space.

Since National Gallery Singapore is a building that houses Singapore's Former Supreme Court and City Hall, the exterior gives a profound impression, yet, oddly, there is no authoritarian atmosphere. One reason for this is the space for children located directly in the middle of the gallery.

According to Deputy Director (Education) Ye Shufang, given the awareness that "children are creative beings," they are aiming for a "diverse and inclusive future" that supports these children. "Diverse" and "inclusive" are keywords frequently heard in Japan as well and can be considered a common universal trend.　(Ayako Naka)

事例3-1 "地域ならでは"のみんなの居場所

三鷹市星と森と絵本の家

　三鷹市星と森と絵本の家は、国立天文台の森の中にある大正時代の建物を保存活用し、絵本の展示や絵本を楽しむ場の提供、自然や科学への関心につながる活動を行っている。館長の鈴木範子さんと、2009年の開館以来運営に携わっている主任の谷口哲さんにお話を伺った。

　開設の経緯について、鈴木さんは次のように語る。「三鷹市は図書館活動、文庫活動が盛んな文化的土壌があり、2005年、市が掲げた『絵本館構想』についてさまざまなかたちで市民との対話を重ねました。絵本を通しての交流や施策の展開には賛同を集めたものの、『館』（建物）の必要性に疑問の声もあり、市内全域で絵本を通してこどもを育む視点を広げていく『みたか・子どもと絵本プロジェクト』として方向を転換し、建物ありきではない活動をしてきました。一方、国立天文台との連携協働のなかで、大正4年建築の旧1号官舎を保存活用し、絵本と体験活動を通じてこどもたちの科学への関心の基礎に働きかける活動を行うことが決まり、『みたか・子どもと絵本プロジェクト』の特色ある活動拠点としての『星と森と絵本の家』が開設されたのです。」

旧官舎の外観 | The exterior of the old official residence

Case3-1 A place "unique to the community" where everyone belongs
Mitaka Picture Book House in the Astronomical Observatory Forest

Mitaka Picture Book House in the Astronomical Observatory Forest is a renovated building from the Taisho period (1912-1926) located in the middle of the forest that houses the National Astronomical Observatory of Japan (NAOJ). The facility offers picture book exhibitions, a place to enjoy picture books, and conducts activities that lead children to become interested in nature and science. I interviewed Director Noriko Suzuki and Manager Satoru Taniguchi, who has handled operations since the facility opened in 2009.

Suzuki says the following of the circumstances of the facility's founding. "Mitaka is a city with a cultural foundation ripe with library- and book-related activities, and in 2005, a series of discussions were held in various forms with city residents on the topic of 'The Conception of a Picture Book House.' While most agreed with the development of picture book-based exchanges and programs, there were doubts as to the necessity of a 'house' (building). Therefore, the project changed direction, becoming the 'Mitaka Children and Picture Book Project,' which aimed to expand the perspectives of educating children through picture books in areas all around the city and did not necessitate a building. Meanwhile, with the coordination and cooperation of the NAOJ,

自然豊かな中庭｜The inner garden abundant with nature

来館者との隠れた対話に応える

　旧官舎の建物は、畳敷きの客間や居間、長い廊下や縁側など、大正・昭和の時代にタイムスリップしたかのような雰囲気を醸し出している。どのようなこだわりをもって空間づくりをしているのだろうか。

「絵本の家では、図鑑や絵本などさまざまな本を、『星』『森』『ひと・くらし』など独自の分類テーマに従って展示しています。また、夏は昆虫、秋は木の実など、その季節に合ったテーマの本を集めて手に取りやすいところに置いています」と鈴木さんは言う。本棚に並ぶ約2500冊の本は、家の中ならどこでも自由なところで読むことができる。かつて浴室だった場所は、今はままごとなどのおもちゃであそべる場所になっている。また、古いミシンや火鉢などが置いてありどこか懐かしい温かな気持ちにもさせられる。ここでは、親子だけではなく、大人たちだけでものんびりと過ごしている。ひとりで本を手に取ったり、地域の高齢者の方が昔を懐かしんだりこどもたちの姿を眺めたり。決して広くはないが、それぞれが思い思いに過ごしている。

　企画展示コーナーの展示物は、ほとんどが手作りの展示だ。「絵本と科学の結びつきを考え、小さい子でもわかるように企画をしています。日々の来館者の行動をみていて、もっとこうしたらわかりやすいな、と説明を足したり、わかりにくい部分を直したり、位置を調整したりしています。1年ごとの企画展ですが、何度も手を入れて、すこしずついいものになっている。手作りだからこそ、変化をもたせることができていると思います」と語る谷口さんは、興味をひき、よりわかりやすい展示づくりのための手間を惜しまない。

it was decided to renovate the old No. 1 official residence constructed in Taisho 4 (1915) and use it to conduct activities that encourage children to form an interest in science through picture books and hands-on experiences. Hence, the Mitaka Picture Book House in the Astronomical Observatory Forest was founded as a distinctive activity base for the Mitaka Children and Picture Book Project.

Responding to unspoken discussions with visitors

With its tatami-covered parlor and sitting room, its long hallways, and its open veranda, the old official residence building projects an aura as if one has gone back in time to the Taisho or Showa (1926-1988) period. What was the focus when creating this space?

According to Suzuki, "The picture book house displays a variety of books including illustrated guides and picture books that follow unique categorized themes such as 'the stars,' 'the forest,' and 'people and lifestyles.' It also collects books with seasonal themes such as 'insects' in the summer and 'nuts and berries' in the fall and keeps them within easy reach." The roughly 2,500 books lining the shelves can be read freely anywhere inside the house. A place that was once the bathroom now has toys and is somewhere that children can play house. Furthermore, accouterments such as an old sewing machine and charcoal brazier somehow elicit a warm sense of nostalgia. Here, one can find not only children, but also adults relaxing on their own. Adults pick up books themselves, and elderly community residents reminisce about the past while watching the children. While the space is not large by any means, each visitor spends time in his or her own way.

The exhibition pieces in the special exhibition corner are mostly hand-made. "We considered the connection between picture books and science, and we designed it so

さまざまな本が並ぶ読書室
The reading corner filled with a variety of books

みんなでつくる、みんなの居場所

　豊かな自然が広がる中庭では、落ち葉やどんぐりを拾ったり、竹馬であそんだり、こどもたちが青空の下のびのびと過ごすことができる。中庭での活動について、鈴木さんはこう語る。

「『森のクラフト』という木工コーナーが人気です。ここでは、ボランティアスタッフがさまざまな工作のアイテムを考えて活動して下さっています。また、小中学生のボランティアスタッフもいて、お月見会や七夕のお祭りのなかで、模擬店やきもだめしなど、こども目線で楽しめる企画を主体的に立案し、絵本の家の活動を支える担い手として活躍しています。」

　谷口さんは、「はっけんコーナー」について教えてくれた。

「庭には『はっけんノート』を置いていて、みんなが発見したこと、みつけたものや感想などを自由にかいています。いろいろな気づきがかき込まれていて、毎年製本し、保管しています。こどもにとってはささいなことも大発見ですよね。こどもの興味関心に寄り添っていきたいです。」

　庭で育った植物で染めたという草木染を使って装丁された「はっけんノート」には、こどもだけでなく大人のかき込みも多く、さまざまな人がここで楽しみ、発見した足跡が残されている。

　こどもたちの未来について谷口さんにお話を伺うと、「こども自身がどんな人物になりたいのかを考えてほしいです。身近に尊敬できる人がいて育っていく環境、地域、人間関係があるといいですよね。私たちはここで体験や交流も提供しているので、その役割の重要性を感じていつも試行錯誤しています」と、温かい笑顔で話してくれた。この、ほっとする温かな空間には運営している人たちの思いが詰まっている。そして、スタッフとここでの活動に参加する人たちとともに、星と森と絵本の家も成長を続けている。

（井部玲子）

中庭の「はっけんコーナー」
The "Discovery Corner" in
the inner garden

that even small children can understand the concepts. We watch the actions of our visitors every day and add explanations that we think would make certain ideas easier to understand, fix parts that are hard to understand, and adjust the positions of things. The exhibition is changed annually, and we continue to make additions and gradually improve it. I think we have been successful in making changes because of its hand-made nature," says Taniguchi, who clearly spares no effort in creating an exhibit that is interesting and easier to understand.

A place made by everyone, for everyone

In the inner garden, abundant with rich nature, children can collect fallen leaves and acorns, play with stilts, and have a relaxing time under the blue sky. Suzuki says the following of the activities held in the inner garden.

"Our 'Forest Craft' woodworking corner is popular. Here, our volunteer staff think of a variety of construction items that can be used for different activities. There are also elementary school and middle school student volunteer staff who independently plan projects that are enjoyable from children's perspectives, such as snack stands and tests of courage. In this way, they act as leaders in supporting the activities of the picture book house."

Taniguchi told me about the "Discovery Corner."

"In the garden there is a 'Discovery Corner' where children can freely write about what they discovered, what they found, their impressions, and more. The many discoveries recorded here are bound into a book each year and saved. For children, even the smallest thing is a big discovery. I want to take into account the interests of children."

These "Discovery Notebooks," which are bound using plant dyes from the plants that grow in the garden, are filled with writings from adults as well as children, a reminder of the various visitors who had fun and made discoveries.

When I asked Taniguchi about the future for children, he said with a warm smile, "I want children to think about what kind of people they want to become. It is good for them to have people they admire nearby and an environment, a community, and relationships to grow up with. Since we provide hands-on experiences and exchanges here, we feel the importance of that role and we are continually engaged in a process of trial and error." This warm, relaxing space is filled with the sentiments of the people that operate it. Along with the staff and those who participate in the facility's activities, Mitaka Picture Book House in the Astronomical Observatory Forest continues to grow.

(Reiko Ibe)

概要 Summary

三鷹市星と森と絵本の家
三鷹市大沢 2 丁目 21 番 3 号　国立天文台内
Mitaka Picture Book House in the Astronomical Observatory Forest
2-21-3 Osawa, National Astronomical Observatory of Japan (NAOJ), Mitaka City, Tokyo
http://www.city.mitaka.tokyo.jp/ehon/

事例3-2 "みんなで子育て"を支える行政と企業の協働の場
八王子市親子つどいの広場 ゆめきっず

　ゆめきっずは、2012年に八王子市、株式会社ボーネルンド、JR東京西駅ビル開発株式会社の3者による「八王子こそだての森事業」に関する協定にもとづき、セレオ八王子北館6階に設置された子育て支援施設だ。ゆめきっずの設立経緯とその後の展開について、八王子市、ボーネルンド、ゆめきっずの現場の方々にお話を伺った。

「どこの市でも子育ての取り組みをしているが、八王子市は子育てしやすいまちNo.1を目指している」と子どものしあわせ課課長の平塚裕之さんは語った。ちなみにこの部署名は、2008年に子ども議会で中学生により命名されたという。このことからも子育てに対して本気で取り組む八王子市の姿勢が伝わってくる。さて、どうすればNo.1になれるのだろうか。「オール八王子ではじめて子育てしやすいまちが生まれる」と平塚さんは言葉をつないだ。社会全体で子育てを支えるという方針のもと、ゆめきっずのような行政と企業とのコラボレーションに加え、地域の中のひとつひとつの店舗との連携をも視野に入れているという。

　しかし、はじめからうまくいっていたわけではない。かつて八王子市在住の母親たちと意見交換した際にはあまりよい評価は得られていなかった。むしろ、他の市を羨んで

3歳までを対象とした八王子市親子つどいの広場ゆめきっず | Hachioji City Playground for Children and Parents Yume Kids, aimed at children up to three years old ©キドキドセレオ八王子店／KID-O-KID CELEO HACHIOJI

Case3-2 A place where the government and businesses cooperate to support "community child-raising""

Hachioji City Playground for Children and Parents Yume Kids

Yume Kids is a child-raising support facility established in 2012 on the sixth floor of the CELEO HACHIOJI North Building as a collaboration between Hachioji City, BørneLund Corporation, and JR Tokyo West Station Building Development Co., Ltd. under the "Hachioji Child-Rearing Forest Project." I interviewed the people who work on-site at Hachioji City, BørneLund, and Yume Kids about the circumstances of Yume Kids' founding and its subsequent development.

Hiroyuki Hiratsuka, chief of the Children's Happiness Section, said, "While every city implements efforts to support child-raising, Hachioji aims to be the number one easiest city in which to raise children." This section was named by middle school students in a 2008 children's assembly. This is another way in which Hachioji's attitude of implementing serious child-raising efforts comes across. So, how does the city become number one? Hiratsuka added, "A city in which it is easy to raise children will only be born with the entire city of Hachioji working together as one." Based on a policy of society as a whole supporting child-raising, he says that, in addition to collaborations

いる声も聞かれた。しかし、よく話を聞くと、八王子市のサービスを知ってもらえていなかったことがわかった。そこで、八王子市の子育てに関する地域資源を知ってもらうために、SNSなどの情報発信に力を入れるようになった。いまや「八王子市といえば子育てプロモーション」と明言できる状況だ。

こどもの場所とともに、大人も落ち着ける場所を目指して

　ゆめきっずは、キドキドに隣接している。子育て中の方の多くは、キドキドという名前を聞いたことがあるだろう。こどもたちに人気の室内あそび場だ。ゆめきっずは3歳までの低年齢層を対象にしているが、キドキドは6ヵ月から12歳までを対象としている。ゆめきっずとキドキドの間は見通しがよく、こどもたちはキドキドにあるカラフルなアトラクションに惹きつけられて、1歳半くらいからキドキドに移動するケースが多いそうだ。「キドキドには遊具がたくさんあり、体を動かしてあそべる場所でもあるのでお子さんの月齢が上がるにつれ、利用する方が増えていきますね」とゆめきっずを担当する木村広美さんは語った。木村さんのまなざしは、こどもはもとより親へ向いている。「ここは、お子さんのあそぶ場所ですが、保護者も話をしたり、相談をしたり、気軽に来ていただければと思います。そういう保護者が集える居場所はお子さんの居場所より少ないのです」と問題点を指摘したうえで、「何ヵ月から行っていいですか、という質問をよくいただきますが、何ヵ月でもいいですよ、保護者のみなさんの居場所と

1歳未満の赤ちゃんを対象とした親子イベント｜A child-parent event aimed at babies under one year old
©キドキドセレオ八王子店／KID-O-KID CELEO HACHIOJI

between the government and businesses, such as Yume Kids, the city is looking into collaborations between each retailer in the area.

However, this did not go as planned from the beginning. On one occasion in which mothers living in Hachioji exchanged opinions, feedback was negative. In fact, some people envied other cities. However, after listening to the residents, the city found that they had simply not been aware of the services offered by the city of Hachioji. Accordingly, more efforts were put into sharing information on social media and similar platforms to raise awareness on the community child-raising resources that Hachioji offered. Today, Hachioji can boast that it is one the first places equated with child-raising promotion.

Aiming for a place for children where adults can also relax

Yume Kids is located next to KID-O-KID. Most parents who are raising children in Japan have probably heard of KID-O-KID, an indoor play area that is popular with children. While Yume Kids' target demographic is small children up to 3 years old, KID-O-KID targets children from 6 months to 12 years old. There is a clear view between Yume Kids and KID-O-KID, so that children are drawn to KID-O-KID's colorful attractions, and many move to KID-O-KID once they turn 18 months old. According to Hiromi Kimura of Yume Kids, "KID-O-KID has lots of play equipment and it is also a place where children can move around a lot to play, so the number of users increases as children get older." Kimura's gaze is aimed at both the children and the parents. She next pointed out a problem: "This is a place for children to play, but we also want the guardians to talk, consult with us, and feel that they can come here without hesitation. Places like that where the guardians can gather and feel welcome are less common than places for children." She followed this with, "I often get asked, 'How old does my child have to be to start coming here?' and I say, 'Any age is fine.' I convey to the guardians that I want them to use this facility as a place where they can come and stay." Kimura expressed a belief that if parents are in a relaxed state without stress, it will change the way they interact with their children.

Support for mothers and fathers

Lastly, I asked about the situation surrounding children and parents. According to Shigeki Makishima, the manager of KID-O-KID, "Recently, there has been an increase in families where both parents work. We want to do all that we can to support parents who bring their children here in order to communicate with them for the limited time they have on their days off. We also see mothers and fathers that stand out because they are not used to playing with their children and are unsure how to do so. It is our job to support those parents as well." It is the close monitoring of parent-child interactions on site that allows considerations to be taken for mothers and fathers as well as the children. I learned that, when creating an environment for children, it is important to

6ヵ月から12歳までを対象としたキドキド｜KID-O-KID, aimed at children between 6 months and 12 years old
©キドキドセレオ八王子店／KID-O-KID CELEO HACHIOJI

して利用してほしいと伝えています」と語った。親がストレスなく落ち着いた状態であれば、こどもに対する向き合い方も変わるという木村さんの信念が伺える。

パパ、ママに対する支援を

最後に、こどもと親をとりまく状況について伺った。キドキドの店長の巻島栄樹さんは、「近頃は共働きの家庭が増加しています。休日の限られた時間を使って親子のコミュニケーションをとりに来られる方を全力で応援したいと思っています。またふだんからこどもとあそび慣れていないために、どうやってあそんであげればいいのかわからないといったパパ、ママも目立ちます。そういった方を支援するのもわれわれの役割です」と教えてくれた。現場の親子の様子をよくみているからこそ、こどもだけでなく、パパやママの状況を気遣うことができる。こどもの環境づくりには、こどもだけでなく、まわりの家族を含めて考えることが重要だと教えてくれた。

現場の親子の様子をよく見ること。これは、八王子市の子育て支援策の原点ともいえる。たとえば、八王子市が日本で初めて本格的に実施した市民向けベビーカーレンタルサービスは、バス利用が多い八王子市民の声から実現した。ママとこどもが外出する際に、ベビーカーではバスに乗りにくいため抱っこひもで外出したものの、目的地に着く前にこどもが寝てしまい、寝た子を抱きかかえたままでは買い物にしにくく、あきらめて帰宅するケースがあったという。外出先でベビーカーを借りることができれば、市民も目的を果たせるし、市内も活性化する。最近では、パパがこどもと自転車で市内に出てきて、外出先でベビーカーを借りて買い物を楽しむケースもあるそうだ。八王子市では、行政と企業がともにパパやママの状況を丁寧に見つめながら、子育てを支援している。

（仲　綾子）

ゆめキッズとキドキドの配置 | Layouts of Yume Kids and KID-O-KID ©ボーネルンド／BORNELUND

consider not only the children themselves, but the families around them.

Keeping a close eye on the interactions between children and parents on site. This can be considered the cornerstone of Hachioji's child-raising support policy. For example, Hachioji's stroller rental service for city residents, the first of its kind to be officially implemented in Japan, came from an idea raised by a city resident who frequently rode the bus. This person cited cases where mothers would go out with their children using baby carriers because it would be too difficult to get on and off of the bus with a stroller. However, the child would fall asleep before reaching their destination and because it would be too hard to shop while carrying the sleeping child, they would give up and return home. If city residents could borrow strollers at their destination, they would be able to fulfill their objective while bringing more life to the city. Recently, there are also cases where fathers come into the city with their children on bicycles, borrow a stroller at their destination, and enjoy shopping. In Hachioji, the government and businesses work together to support child-raising while keeping a close eye on the situations faced by mothers and fathers.

(Ayako Naka)

| 概要 Summary

八王子市親子つどいの広場 ゆめきっず
東京都八王子市旭1-1 セレオ八王子北館6階
Hachioji City Playground for Children and Parents Yume Kids
1-1 Asahi, CELEO Hachioji North Building 6th floor, Hachioji City, Tokyo

http://www.city.hachioji.tokyo.jp/tantoumadoguchi/015/007/001/p001579.html

事例3-3 親子に寄り添う"地域のみんなで子育て"の起点

横浜市 青葉区地域子育て支援拠点 ラフール

　横浜市にある青葉区地域子育て支援拠点 ラフール（以下、ラフール）は、東急田園都市線青葉台駅から歩いて3分、0歳から未就学児とその家族、妊婦さんとその家族、子育ての支援者のための施設である。こどもを安心して産み育てられる地域づくりを目標に、横浜市が各区に1カ所ずつ整備している地域子育て支援拠点のひとつだ。横浜市青葉区役所子ども家庭支援課の横田慈係長、溝渕奈央さん同席のもと、施設長の山田範子さんにお話を伺った。

　「ラフールは、青葉区の委託を受けてNPO法人ワーカーズ・コレクティブ パレットが区との協働で運営しています。区とNPOとが協力して活動しているところが特徴です。『ひろば』だけではなく、子育て相談や人材育成など、活動は多岐にわたっています（図1参照）。横浜市内の地域子育て支援拠点が担う役割は同じですが、それぞれの地域の特性に合わせて運営をしています。」

こどものあそび場だが、こどものためだけの場所ではない

　インタビューに伺ったとき、離乳食をテーマにしたおしゃべり会がちょうど終わった

左：授乳室のサイン／右：外あそびが楽しめるテラス　Left: Sign for the Nursing Room / Right: The terrace, where children can play outside

Case3-3 A center for "regional community child-raising" that empathizes with children and parents

City of Yokohama Aoba Childcare Support Center Lafull

Aoba Childcare Support Center Lafull in Yokohama (referred to below as "Lafull") is a facility for children from 0 years of age to preschool age and their families, expectant mothers and their families as well as those who support child-raising. It is a three-minute walk from Aobadai Station on the Tokyu Den-en-toshi Line. It is one of the community childcare support centers that have been built in each ward of Yokohama with the purpose of creating a community where children can be born and raised with peace of mind. I interviewed Facility Director Noriko Yamada, who was also joined by Megumi Yokota, Manager of the Aoba Ward Administration Office Children and Families Support Division and Nao Mizobuchi, from the same division.

"Lafull was commissioned by Aoba Ward and is operated by the ward in cooperation with Workers' Collective Palette, an NPO. One of its distinguishing features is that it operates through the cooperation of the ward and an NPO. In addition to the "plaza," it conducts a wide range of activities including child-raising consultations, cultivation of human resources, etc. (see Fig. 1). Each community childcare support center in the city of

ひろば Plaza	0歳から未就学児や妊婦さんとその家族が、地域の親子や異なる世代の人と交流できる「広場」を開催する A "plaza" is available where children from 0 years of age to preschool age, expectant mothers, and their families can interact with other children and parents in the community as well as people from different generations.
子育て相談 Child-RaisingConsultations	広場内や相談室でスタッフや相談員による子育てに関する相談、電話による相談・情報提供を行う Consultations, phone consultations, and information-sharing on child-raising are conducted by staff and consultants in the plaza and consultation room.
情報の収集と提供 Collection and Provision of Information	青葉区内の子育て家庭に関する情報の収集と提供を行う。ラフールニュースなどの紙面やホームページ、情報コーナーも整備 Lafull collects and provides information on child-raising families in Aoba Ward. It also provides Lafull News and other paper-based information sources as well as a website and information corner.
ネットワーク Networking	地域で子育てを支え合う「人と人のつながり」をつくる Lafull creates "connections between people" so that the community as a whole provides child-raising support.
人材の育成 Cultivation of Human Resources	子育てに関する研修会や講座等を開催したり、子育てサークル活動の支援も行う Lafull holds workshops, lectures, etc. on child-raising and supports the activities of child-raising clubs.
横浜子育てサポートシステム Yokohama Child-Raising Support System	地域でのこどもの預かり合いをサポートする Lafull helps community members look after each other's children.
横浜子育てパートナー Yokohama Child-Raising Partner	子育て期の悩みごとや困りごとの相談を受け、必要な情報を提供し、支援につながるまでサポートする Lafull welcomes consultations from parents about their anxieties and problems during their child-raising period, provides them with necessary information, and supports them until they have the assistance they require.

図1　ラフール7つの役割　　　　　　　　　　　※パンフレットをもとに作成 Based on pamphlet
Fig.1 Lafull's Seven Roles

ところで、赤ちゃん連れのママたちが輪になって和やかな雰囲気で過ごしていた。ここでは、子育て中のパパ・ママが知り合うきっかけとなるプログラムも多く行われている。また、赤ちゃん連れのママだけではなく、パパやおじいちゃん・おばあちゃんとこどもでの利用も多いという。母子以外でも気軽に来てもらえるように工夫がされているのだが、プログラムだけではなく、空間づくりにも工夫をこらしているのがラフールの特徴だ。

「こどもだけを意識したあそび場ではなく、できるだけ大人も過ごしやすく、明るく、清潔感のある空間を目指しました。サインもそのようなデザインで統一しています。また、2歳以上の子や園児さんも来やすくなるように、ロープネットを昇り降りする『探検の木』をつくったり、テラスを開放して縄跳びや缶ぽっくりであそべるようにしています。」

ひろばは「赤ちゃんコーナー」と「動いて遊べるコーナー」、「静かに遊べるコーナー」とに分かれており、大人のためのカフェコーナーも設置されている（図2参照）。また、ベンチを兼ねた木製のパーテーションがその時々で空間を区切るのに使われており、空間のアクセントにもなっている。「実は、当初は廊下のスペースがもったいない

Yokohama plays the same role, but they operate in accordance with the characteristics of each community."

It's a play area for children, but it's not just a place for children

When I arrived for the interview, a discussion session on baby food had just ended, and mothers with babies were sat in a circle in a relaxed atmosphere. The center holds many programs that serve as opportunities to bring together mothers and fathers who are currently raising children. In addition to mothers with babies, it is also frequently used by fathers, grandfathers, and grandmothers with children. It features creative ideas that enable people besides mothers and children to freely visit, and it is distinguished not only by its programs, but also by the ingenuity in the way it created the space inside.

"We aimed for a bright, clean space that was not only a play area with children in mind, but one where adults could also be comfortable. The signs were also standardized with that design. Furthermore, we made it easier for children two and older as well as kindergarten and nursery school children to visit the center by creating the "Exploration Tree" where they can climb up and down a climbing net. We also opened up the terrace so that children can do things such as jump rope and play with can stilts."

The plaza is divided into the "Baby Corner," the "Move & Play Corner," and the "Quiet

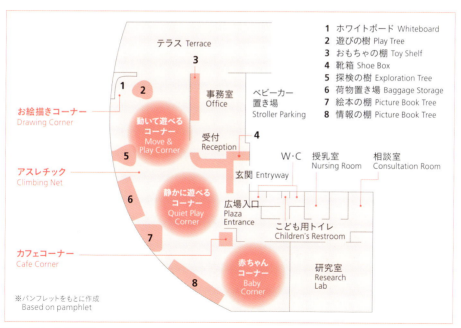

1 ホワイトボード Whiteboard
2 遊びの樹 Play Tree
3 おもちゃの棚 Toy Shelf
4 靴箱 Shoe Box
5 探検の樹 Exploration Tree
6 荷物置き場 Baggage Storage
7 絵本の棚 Picture Book Tree
8 情報の棚 Picture Book Tree

テラス Terrace
3
お絵描きコーナー Drawing Corner
1 2
事務室 Office
ベビーカー置き場 Stroller Parking
動いて遊べるコーナー Move & Play Corner
受付 Reception
4
W・C
授乳室 Nursing Room
相談室 Consultation Room
アスレチック Climbing Net
5
玄関 Entryway
静かに遊べるコーナー Quiet Play Corner
6
広場入口 Plaza Entrance
こども用トイレ Children's Restroom
カフェコーナー Cafe Corner
7
赤ちゃんコーナー Baby Corner
研究室 Research Lab
8
※パンフレットをもとに作成 Based on pamphlet

図2 ラフールのフロア
Fig.2 Lafull Floor Plan

と思っていました。しかし、ヒートアップしてしまったこどものクールダウンの場になったり、ママの気分転換の場になったり、ベンチを置いたので離乳食やおやつをあげる場として使われたり、思いのほか活用されているようです」と山田さんは笑顔で語る。こどもが安全に楽しく過ごせることはもちろんだが、こどもを連れてくる大人たちが、ほっとできる空間であることもとても大事にされている。

「私たちが子育てをしていた時と同じことで悩まないような社会に」

こどもが思うように育たないと、親はそれが自分のせいだと考えてしまいがちだ。地域子育て支援拠点であるラフールにも悩みを抱えた大人が日々訪れる。「こどもも一人ひとり人格があり、違っているのですから、それは当たり前のこと。ひとりで抱え込まないで、思いつめないで、もっと楽に考えてほしいですね」と山田さんは寄り添う。

「私たちが子育てをしていた時に不便だったことを次の世代の人にも不便だと思わせないような、同じことで悩まないような社会にしていきたいと考えています。これからも時代の変化にともなって出てくる新しい悩みを、すこしずつ改善していきたいです。どうしたらもっと子育てしやすいか、ラフールの中だけでなく、地域、青葉区、日本中が子育てしやすくなってほしいと思うと、本当に、終わりがありません。」

山田さんが見据える未来は、誰もが子育てしやすいと思えるような世の中だ。そこに向かって、できることをひとつずつ積み重ねてきた子育ての大先輩からの、重みのある言葉である。

インタビューに伺ったひろばでは、スタッフの方たちの優しい笑顔や声掛けの様子がとても印象的だった。みんなのために工夫をこらした空間があり、そこで温かく迎えてくれるスタッフがいる。ここでは、人も、空間も、訪れるすべての人にやさしく寄り添っている。

（井部玲子）

広くはないがさまざまな用途で使われている廊下。ベンチの奥には、おむつ替え用のベッドがある｜The hallway, while not large, is used for a variety of purposes. Past the benches is a bed for changing diapers

Play Corner." It also includes a Cafe Corner for adults (see Fig. 2) . In addition, wooden partitions that also serve as benches are used to divide the spaces at different times while also serving as an accent to the space. "Actually, I initially thought that the hallway space would be wasted. However, I hear that it is being utilized as a cool-down space for children who become overactive, a place for moms to get a change of scenery, a place to feed children snacks on the benches that are placed there, and other unexpected uses," said Yamada with a smile. While importance is naturally placed on children having a safe, fun experience, it is also placed on providing a space where the adults who bring them can relax.

"Creating a society where parents don't have the same worries that we had when we were raising children"

When parents cannot raise their children the way they expect, they tend to blame themselves. As a community childcare support center, Lafull also sees its daily share of anxiety-filled adults. Yamada empathizes, "Each child has his or her own personality and is different. This is totally natural. I want parents to be more laid back rather than bearing the whole load by themselves and tormenting themselves."

"We want to create a society in which the next generation will not experience the same inconveniences that we did or have the same anxieties we did when we were raising children. We want to gradually rectify the new anxieties that arise with the changing times. If we think about how we can make child-raising easier not just within Lafull, but in the community, in Aoba Ward, and in Japan, then there is really no end."

The future that Yamada envisions is one in which everyone will think that it is easy to raise a child. These are words that carry a lot of weight, spoken by a senior and mentor in child-raising who has done everything that she can to make that a reality.

I was impressed by the kind smiles and greetings of the staff members in the plaza where I conducted the interview. There was a space that was well-devised for everyone and staff who warmly welcome all the visitors. At this center, the people and the space gently support everyone who comes here.

(Reiko Ibe)

▎概要 Summary
横浜市 青葉区地域子育て支援拠点 ラフール 横浜市青葉区青葉台 1-4 6F
City of Yokohama Aoba Childcare Support Center Lafull 1-4 Aobadai, 6th floor, Aoba-ku, Yokohama City
http://lafull.net/

こどもも大人も尊重し合える、
"いいかげん" なまちのお茶の間
岡さんのいえ TOMO

A "carefree" town living room where
both children and adults can practice mutual respect
Okasan's house TOMO

　岡さんのいえTOMO は、東京都世田谷区内で良好な環境の形成とまちづくりを推進する「財団法人 世田谷トラストまちづくり」が支援する「地域共生のいえ」のひとつで、オーナーの小池良実さんが地域のこどもたちのために開放している。駄菓子屋などさまざまなプログラムが行われているが、ここでは"見守り隊"とこどもたちの関わりとその環境について紹介したい。

　"見守り隊"は大学院生と定年退職後の男性たちだ。大学院生たちは、社会教育学を専門とする教授の指示で、当初はなかば強制されてここに来たが、何度か来るうちに顔を覚えてもらい、こどもに認められてうれしいから通い続けているという。一方、定年退職後の男性たちは、現役時代は雑誌の編集長や企業の要職に就いていた方々だ。ここでは「偽じじ」の愛称で親しまれ、こどもたちとあそんでいる。知識や経験がある者が年少者に教えるという関係ではなく、互いに個として認め合うことに価値を見出して集まっている。

　このような関係を支える環境は、畳、障子、ちゃぶ台といった昔ながらの佇まいをもつ一軒家だ。この家が次世代を支える拠点になる。小池さんの願いは「ここのにぎやかなこどもたちが大人になって岡さんのいえのスタッフになればいい」ということだ。うまく世代交代できれば、このような関係を支える環境が生まれ続けるだろう。そのために大事なことは「適当さ、いいかげんは良い加減って言いますしね」と小池さんは言う。どこか懐かしく、抜けがある日本家屋は、"いいかげん"を支える環境としてふさわしい。(仲 綾子)

こども、親、見守り隊。多世代が集う居間｜Children, parents, and the "Watch Guard." The living room where many generations gather ©岡さんのいえTOMO／Okasan's house TOMO

Okasan's house TOMO is one of several "Community Symbiosis Houses" supported by Setagaya Trust & Community Design, a foundation that promotes the formation of good environments and the building of communities within the Setagaya ward of Tokyo. The house's owner, Kazumi Koike opened it to the public for local children. While the house holds a variety of programs such as a traditional candy store, I would like to introduce the "Watch Guard," its involvement with children, and its environment.

The "Watch Guard" is a group of graduate students and retired men. The graduate students initially came here half-forced under the instruction of their educational sociology professor, but after coming several times, they were happy that the children recognized their faces and acknowledged them, so they continued to come back. The retired men used to work as chief editors of magazines or at important company positions. They are affectionately known here as "fake grandpas" as they play with the children. Rather than those with knowledge and experience teaching the younger generation, they get together and find value in acknowledging one another as individuals.

The environment that supports such a relationship is an old-fashioned single-family house with tatami flooring, sliding screen doors, and traditional chabudai low tables. This house is a center that supports the next generation. It is Koike's wish that "the lively children who come here grow up to become staff of Okasan's house." As long as the generational "changing of the guard" goes well, the house will continue to foster an environment that supports such relationships. According to Koike, "half-heartedness" is important. After all, the Japanese word for iikagen ("carefree") literally means "just the right level." This somehow nostalgic, open Japanese house is the perfect environment to support a "carefree" atmosphere.

(Ayako Naka)

©JRCMC

事例4-1 赤ちゃんにやさしい病院の大きな窓

日本赤十字社医療センター 周産母子センター

　日本赤十字社医療センターの周産母子センターは、産科と新生児医療を統合して2010年に誕生した。ここは、世界保健機関（WHO）とユニセフが認定する「赤ちゃんにやさしい病院（ベビーフレンドリーホスピタル）」のひとつとしてよく知られている。つまり、母乳育児に積極的に取り組む施設として有名だ。周産母子センターの計画上の留意点と今後の展望について、看護副部長の井本寛子さんと看護師長の中根直子さんにお話を伺った。

　周産母子センターの計画でとくによく考えた点について伺ったところ、「光を採り入れること、広い空間を確保すること、直接目に光が入らない照明、足にやさしい床、気がかりにならない色、こどもの視線の高さ、ソファの座面の高さ……」と、井本さんは迷いなく次々と挙げてくれた。誇れる点がたくさんあることだけでなく、竣工後、数年過ぎてもなお、計画当時の思いがまるで今のことのように語られることに驚いた。計画時の思いは、日々の活動のなかで確実に継承されている。挙げていただいた点すべてを紹介したいところだが、紙面の都合上、ここでは「光を採り入れること」について取り上げたい。

大きな窓と間接照明からの柔らかい光に満ちた授乳サロン　A nursing salon filled with soft light from the large window and ambient lighting ©JRCMC

`Case4-1` Large windows at a baby-friendly hospital
Japanese Red Cross Medical Center Perinatal/Pediatric Center

The Japanese Red Cross Medical Center Perinatal/Pediatric Center was created in 2010 by integrating the maternity ward and neonatal care. It is well known as one of several "baby-friendly hospitals" certified by the World Health Organization (WHO) and UNICEF. In other words, it is famous as a facility that actively supports breastfeeding. I asked Deputy Director of Nursing Hiroko Imoto and Head Nurse Naoko Nakane about the matters taken into consideration when designing the Perinatal/Pediatric Center and its future development.

When I asked about which aspects in particular were closely considered during the planning stage for the Perinatal/Pediatric Center, Imoto gave me the following list without hesitation: bringing in light, maintaining an expansive space, lighting that does not let light directly into people's eyes, a floor that was easy on the feet, colors that do not cause anxiety, consideration of the height of children's sight lines, the height of the sofa seats, etc. I was surprised that she spoke not only in terms of the many things she was proud of, but as if the sentiments that she felt at the time of planning are exactly the same as those she feels now, even several years after its completion. The sentiments that

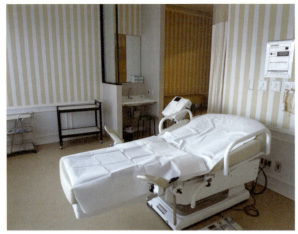

一般分娩室。壁紙の色や柄は部屋ごとに異なる　A general delivery room. The wallpaper colors and patterns differ by room ©JRCMC

光は誰のために？

　周産母子センターのNICU（新生児集中治療室）、GCU（回復期治療室・強化治療室）には採光のための窓がある。このような「厳密な温湿度調整を要する治療室」は「採光のための開口部を要しない」※と法的に採光規定が緩和されており、実際には、窓を設ける事例はあまり多くない。しかし、計画当時にセンター長だった杉本充弘医師の強い意志で大きな窓を設ける方針となった。その理由を「赤ちゃんにとって、ということもあるけれど、むしろ、ここにくるお母さん、お父さん、さらにケアをしている看護師たちにとっての気持ちよさ。それが伝わるから」と井本さんは教えてくれた。こどものまわりの人たちの気持ちは、こどもに伝わる。だから、こどもだけに着目するのではなく、まわりの人たちを視野に入れて計画することが大切だ。

　窓は、分娩室にも授乳サロンにもある。一般的にはお産も授乳もプライベートな行為として閉じたところで行われがちだが、「人間らしく光を浴びながらお産する。生まれてきた赤ちゃんにも光は必要です」と井本さんは指摘した。プライバシーに対する考え方を伺うと、「必要な時にはプライバシーを確保できるようにすればよい。でも、いつも必要なわけではない」と井本さんはさらりと語ったが、この本質をつかんだうえでのしなやかな考え方こそが、窓のある分娩室や授乳サロンというこれまでにない空間を生み出す原点なのだろう。なにか目新しい空間をつくってみようというような表面的な野心は微塵もない。

こどもは未来創造可能性

　最後に、こども、親、未来について、どのように捉えているかを伺うと、井本さんはきっぱりと「こどもは未来創造可能性がある」と語った。未来創造可能性とは何を意味するのだろう。「赤ちゃんのことを無力だと思っていませんか。自分も経験が浅いころは、赤ちゃんに対してなにかしてあげなくてはいけないと思っていました。でも、たと

she felt at that time of are clearly still present and play an active role in daily activities. I wish I could introduce each and every aspect that she mentioned, but due to space restrictions, I will focus on the idea of "bringing in light."

Who is the light for?

The Neonatal Intensive Care Unit (NICU) and Growing Care Unit (GCU) at the Perinatal / Pediatric Center have windows to let in light. For these kinds of "care units that require strict temperature and humidity adjustment," the legal lighting regulations are relaxed in that they "do not require an opening to let in light" [※], and so not many actually have windows installed. However, it was decided to install a large window due to the strong inclination of Dr. Mitsuhiro Sugimoto, who was director of the center in the planning stages. According to Imoto, the reason for this was "for the babies, of course, but also for the comfort of the mothers and fathers who come here as well as the care-giving nurses. Because that feeling is passed on." The feelings of the people around children are passed on to them. Therefore, it is important not to focus solely on the children, but to also consider the people around them when planning.

There are also windows in the delivery rooms and nursing salons. Although delivery and nursing generally tend to be conducted in private, Imoto pointed out the importance of "giving birth while bathed in light like a human being. A newborn baby requires light as well." When I asked how she felt about privacy, she readily answered, "Privacy should be available when necessary, but it is not always necessary." Perhaps it is the flexible approach that comes with grasping the essence of this idea that allows for the creation of such unprecedented spaces as delivery rooms and nursing salons with windows. There is no sign of superficial ambitions to create a fresh, original space.

畳のある分娩室。家族の
待機スペースにもなる
A tatami-floored delivery
room. It is also a waiting
space for families ©JRCMC

天井に青空の絵が描かれたNICU・GCU　The NICU and GCU with ceilings painted like the blue sky　©JRCMC

えどんなに小さくても赤ちゃんには生きる力がある。たとえば、元気な赤ちゃんは大きな声で泣いて主張するけれど、すこし元気がない赤ちゃんは省エネで（無駄なエネルギーを使わずに）なんとかやっている。生きる天才です」と補足してくれた。

　中根さんは「大人とこどもの境界線はあまりないと思う」と意外な言葉をつぶやいたが、意味するところは同じだろう。こどもを「なにかしてあげる対象」として捉えるのではなく、個として尊重している。助産師として長年の経験をもち、多くの赤ちゃんをみてきた井本さん、中根さんだからこそ得られる謙虚な視点だ。

「こどものため」という謳い文句をあちこちでみかけるが、大人がこどものためになにかしてあげるという姿勢にはおごりがあるのかもしれない。この思いを見透かしたように、「こどものためと言いながら、結局、自分のことばかり主張する大人が多い」と井本さんは暗に批判し、「こどものため」という言葉の奥にある本音を見通す力を身につける大切さを教えてくれた。

（仲 綾子）

※　　建設省住宅局建築指導課長通知第一五三号、平成 7 年 5 月25日　　Notice No. 153, Building Guidance Division Chief, Housing Bureau, Ministry of Construction, May 25, 1995

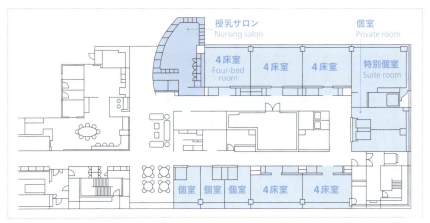

図1　周産母子センター平面図
Fig.1 Perinatal/Pediatric Center floor plan

Children can build the future

Lastly, when I asked how she perceived children, parents, and the future, Imoto said decisively, "Children have the potential to build the future." What does "the potential to build the future" mean? "You probably consider babies as helpless," she added and went on to say, "Back when I was inexperienced, I also thought that babies had to have everything done for them. However, no matter how small they are, babies have the ability to live. For example, healthy babies cry loudly to get attention, but babies that are not quite well conserve energy (do not waste energy) when they do things. They are 'geniuses' when it comes to living."

Nakane murmured the surprising words, "I don't think there are very many dividing lines between adults and children," which probably has a similar meaning. Rather than thinking of children as "needing things to be done for them," they are respected as individuals. Both Imoto and Nakane have many years of experience as midwives and seeing lots of babies, this is what allows for this modest perspective.

The slogan "for the children" is seen in a lot of places, but the attitude that adults should do things for children may be somewhat arrogant. As if she saw through these feelings, Imoto implicitly criticized, "People often say that something is 'for the children' and turn out to be advocating for themselves," showing me the importance of acquiring the ability to see through to the true intent behind the words "for the children."

(Ayako Naka)

┃概要 Summary

日本赤十字社医療センター 周産母子センター 東京都渋谷区広尾 4-1-22
Japanese Red Cross Medical Center Perinatal/Pediatric Center 4-1-22 Hiroo, Shibuya-ku, Tokyo
http://www.med.jrc.or.jp/hospital/clinic/tabid/240/Default.aspx

事例4-2 公園のような病院のホスピタルアート

国立成育医療研究センター 病院

　国立成育医療研究センター 病院は、国立小児病院と国立大蔵病院を統合して2002年に竣工した。病床数は490床。日本で有数の大型こども病院だ。こども病院と書いたが、対象は小児だけではない。成育医療、つまり胎児期から新生児期、乳児期、学童期、思春期を経て成人期まで包括的に見据えた医療を提供している。ここでは高度な専門医療と研究が行われているが、冷たさは感じられない。むしろほっとするような心地よい空間がある。その秘密について、設計者である辻吉隆さんとアートワークを手掛けた吉田祐美さんにお話を伺った。

「病院建築の設計では、複層する医療機能の整合に終始してしまい、本来備えておくべき療養環境の充実までに行きつけていないものが多いよね。療養環境の計画では、自然環境をうまく取り込むことが重要なのだけれど、そこまでのデザインに至らずに駐車場の中に取り残されたような病院をよくみかけるね。それは病院の本質ではないので、このセンターでは敷地の中央に歩行者専用の庭園を設けて、地域と自然と人が豊かに共生できる『ガーデンホスピタル』をつくろうと考えた」と辻さんは語る。たしかにここはまるで公園のようだ。ベビーカーで来たママとパパと赤ちゃんが階段状のベンチに座っ

森の中にいる鳥や動物を表現した木製のアートワーク　Wooden art pieces that depict birds and animals in the forest　©タウンアート／TOWN ART

Case4-2 Hospital art at a park-like hospital
National Center for Child Health and Development Hospital

The National Center for Child Health and Development Hospital was completed in 2002, integrating the National Children's Hospital and National Okura Hospital. With 490 beds, it is a leading large-scale children's hospital in Japan. Although I wrote "children's hospital," its target is not only children. It provides developmental medical care—that is, comprehensive medical care from the prenatal and neonatal periods through infancy, school age, and puberty, all the way up until adulthood. Although highly specialized medical care and research is conducted here, there is no sense of coldness. On the contrary, it is a comfortable, relaxing space. I asked Yoshitaka Tsuji, the architect, and Yumi Yoshida, who handled the artwork, about the secret behind this.

According to Tsuji, "When designing the hospital construction, many people start and end with coordinating the multi-layered medical care functions and never get to the stage of completeness as a medical care environment that should essentially be provided. When designing a medical care environment, it is important to skillfully incorporate the natural environment, but I often see hospitals that don't reach that level of design, making you feel like you have been left in the middle of a parking lot. That is

てくつろいでいる。せせらぎをのぞき込む男の子もいる。

　施設の中に入ると、病院らしくない不思議な仕掛けがあちこちにあることがわかる。この不思議なものは木製の小さな人形、機械仕掛けの怪獣、カラフルなモビールなどだ。今でこそホスピタルアートはよくみられるようになってきたが、竣工当時はめずらしかったことだろう。「合理的な建築だけ、つるんとした空間だけでは、人との対話ができない。アートがあるとそれを介してコミュニケーションがとれる。入院していることもたちに、ひとりじゃないよ、このアートを通じて理解し合える人たちがまわりにいるんだよって伝えたかった」と辻さんは教えてくれた。

　ただ、ここは成育医療を行う場。対象はこどもだけではなく、成人もいる。だから、こどもを惹きつけるだけでなく、大人もじっくり向き合えるようなアートが設置されている。「こども向けだけのアートをつくっても、大人にとってつらい空間になるから」と語る辻さんは、外来診療棟では、乳児、幼児、成人と年齢ごとのエリアにふさわしいアートを配置するように計画した。

アートは共通言語になる

　一方で、こどもにも大人にも共通してアートが果たす役割がある。吉田さんは、「ブルーのあれがあるところでね」とある場所について説明していたユーザーの例を挙げて、「色とかアートとかは、なにかを伝える共通言語になる」と指摘している。ウェイファインディング（目的地にスムーズに導くこと）は、病院においてはとくに重視される考え方だが、アートはこの役割を、押しつけがましくなく、ユーザーが意識しないうちに果たしている。

not the true nature of a hospital, so at this center, we decided to build a pedestrian-only garden in the center of the grounds and create a 'garden hospital' where the community, nature, and people could achieve a rich coexistence." This does indeed resemble a park. Mothers, fathers, and babies who came with strollers sit on the stepped benches and relax. There is also a boy peering into the stream.

Inside the facility, I see that there are strange, un-hospital-like contraptions all around. These strange things include small wooden dolls, mechanical monsters, and colorful mobiles. While hospital art is frequently seen these days, it was probably rare at the time this hospital was completed. Tsuji told me, "With just logical construction, with just a smooth space, people cannot have conversations. When there is art, people can use it as a gateway to communication. I wanted to convey to the hospitalized children that you are not alone, you are surrounded by people with whom you can have a mutual understanding through this art."

However, this is a place where developmental medical care is performed. It is not only for children, but adults as well. For this reason, the hospital displays not only art that draws the eye of children, but that with which adults, too, can interact. "Even if we made art that was solely child-oriented, it would be a difficult place for adults to be," says Tsuji, who designed the outpatient ward so that it would display art that is appropriate for each age group from infants and young children to adults.

Art becomes a common language

On the other hand, art plays a common role for both children and adults. Yoshida

つまみを回すと中の人形が動くアートワーク　An art piece where the doll moves when the lever is turned ©辻吉隆／Yoshitaka Tsuji

緑豊かな公園のような病院　A hospital that resembles a nature-rich park ©辻吉隆／Yoshitaka Tsuji

求められるのは、思いを伝えるしくみづくり

　竣工からおよそ15年が過ぎたいま、国立成育医療研究センターのアートをとりまく状況はすこし変化した。木製のユニークな顔のアートは、みんなが触ってお鼻がツルツルになっている。一方、手を入れてロープをひっぱると蛇が出てくるアートワークは、ロープがちぎれたままになっている。愛され続けるアートがある一方で、メンテナンスされずにいるアートがある。「われわれは企画側だから、どこかで手が離れていく。思いを伝えていくことは難しい」と問題点を挙げたうえで、オリエンテーションや研修などの必要性を吉田さんは指摘する。思いを伝えるしくみづくりが求められている。

　最後に、どのような未来を思い描いているかを伺った。アートを手掛けた吉田さんは「みんながそれぞれ尊重されていける感じがいいなぁ。アートの一番おもしろいところは多様なところだと思います。いろんな風に想像してもらえるとか。これじゃないとだめって感じは嫌だなと思っています」と語った。この言葉は、こどもだけに向けられたものではない。こどもも大人も、おじいちゃんもおばあちゃんも。「ミックスがいい」という吉田さんが見据える射程は広い。設計者の辻さんはニコニコしたまま、何も語らなかった。建築家は空間で伝える、きっとそういう思いがあるのだろう。そして、それは病院を訪れるこどもたちとその家族に伝わっている。

（仲 綾子）

ホスピタルアートを紹介するブックレット　A booklet on hospital art ©タウンアート／TOWN ART

recalled one user that explained a certain location as "the place where that blue thing is," and she pointed out, "Things like color and art become a common language that convey certain things." Wayfinding (smooth guidance to a destination) is an approach that is particularly valued at hospitals, and art fills this role without being intrusive and without users being aware of that fact.

A need to create schemes that convey sentiments

Now that roughly 15 years have passed since completion, the situation surrounding art at the National Center for Child Health and Development has changed slightly. The unique wooden face art has been touched by so many people that the noses are smooth. Meanwhile, on a piece of art where visitors insert their hands and pull on the rope to make a snake come out, the rope lays broken. While some pieces of art continue to be loved, others have not been maintained. "We are the planning side, there comes a point when it is out of our hands. It's hard to continue to convey sentiment," says Yoshida, raising issues while pointing out the necessity of orientations, training, and the like. There is a need to create schemes that convey sentiments.

Lastly, I asked how they imagine the future. Yoshida, who handled the art, said, "It's nice how each person can be respected in his or her own way. I think the most interesting part of art is that it is diverse. That people can interpret it in lots of different ways. I don't like the idea of something having to be a certain way." These words are not aimed only at children. They are for children and adults, grandmothers and grandfathers. Yoshida expressed her open-mindedness, saying, "I prefer a mix." Tsuji, the architect, just smiled and remained silent. He was surely thinking that architects speak through the spaces they create. This is conveyed to the children and their families who visit the hospital

(Ayako Naka)

▌概要 Summary

国立成育医療研究センター 病院 東京都世田谷区大蔵 2-10-1
National Center for Child Health and Development Hospital 2-10-1 Okura, Setagaya-ku, Tokyo
https://www.ncchd.go.jp/

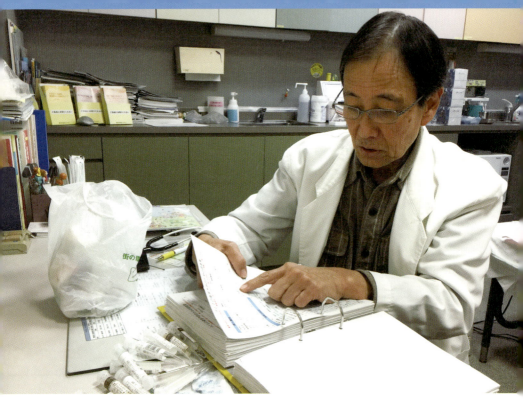

事例4-3 こどもの事故を予防する地域のゲートキーパー

緑園こどもクリニック

　緑園こどもクリニックは、横浜市泉区にある診療所だ。院長の山中龍宏さんが「大学病院や専門病院と比べてクリニック（個人の診療所）は地域の人との接点が多い。だから、病気の診療のほかに、よろず相談も受けるようにしています。学校に行けない子とかね。福祉との接点が大切」と語るように、地域に密着した医療福祉のゲートキーパー（悩んでいる人を見守り、必要な支援につなげる役割）となっている。

　ずっと前から地域になじんでいるかのようにみえる山中さんだが、実は、ここで開業したのは19年前、「自分のスタイルが確立された」と感じていた50歳のときだという。それ以前は、東京大学医学部を卒業後、大学病院やアメリカの研究所などに勤務していた。山中さんに対して、医者という面だけでなく、研究者あるいは教育者という面を感じるのは、そのような背景があるのだろう。

こどもの事故を予防する3つのE、とりわけ環境の重要性

　研究者、教育者という面を最も感じるのは、Safe Kids Japan の活動だ。これは、こどもの事故によるけがを防ぐことを目的として設立されたNPO法人で、山中さんが理

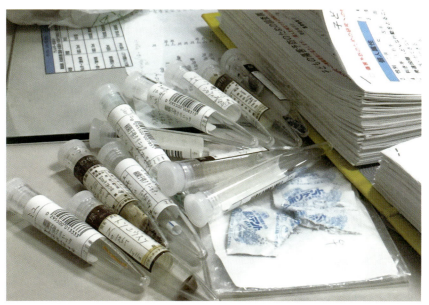

こどもが実際に誤飲したものと記録したカルテ | Items that a child actually swallowed by accident and the medical chart recording the incident

Case4-3 A community gatekeeper that prevents child-related accidents
Ryokuen Children's Clinic

Ryokuen Children's Clinic is a clinic in the Izumi ward of Yokohama. According to Director Tatsuhiro Yamanaka, "Compared to university hospitals and specialized hospitals, private clinics are often a point of contact between people and their community. For this reason, we offer various consultations in addition to diagnosing illnesses, like for children who can't go to school. The point of contact with welfare is important." In this way, the clinic is a gatekeeper (someone who watches over anxious people and leads them to the necessary support) of medical care and welfare in close contact with the community.

Yamanaka seems to have belonged to the community for a long time, but actually, he only opened his clinic here 19 years ago at the age of 50 once he felt he had "established his own style." Before that, after graduating from the University of Tokyo Graduate School of Medicine, he worked at university hospitals and in laboratories in the United States. Perhaps it is this background that made me feel that Yamanaka has a side of him that is a researcher or an educator in addition to that of a doctor.

図1　こどもの事故を予防する3つのE
Fig.1 The 3 E's to Prevent Children's Accidents

事長を務める。どのような経緯ではじめられたのだろうか。

「現場にいると、病気だけでなくけがや事故で来る子もいます。たとえば1歳3カ月の子がやけどをしてしまったり、6カ月の子がシールのようなものをのどに詰まらせてしまったり。このような日常的な事故は医学の教科書には載っていません。」

　このような事故を防ぐ方法として3つのE、つまりEnvironment（環境）、Education（教育）、Enforcement（法律）を変えるというアプローチがある。これらのうち、法律を変えるのは時間がかかる。教育は最もよく行われているが、実際はほとんど効果がないという。なぜ効果がないのだろう。山中さんは「はじめは親の管理が甘いからだと思っていましたが、よく考えれば24時間ずっとこどもから目を離さないでいることは不可能。親がどんなに注意していても、起こるものは起こるのだと思い直しました」と教えてくれた。法律、教育には限界があると感じた山中さんは環境を改善することに注力する。

　環境を改善するためには情報収集が鍵となる。山中さんは事故現場の様子を詳しく記録している。たとえば、「5歳児、転倒、あごを切った」とだけ記録するのではなく、「5歳児がリビングを走っていてラグマットで滑り、高さ50cmのソファの木製の肘掛けであごを切った」と、状況を詳細に記録する。すると、部屋の隅に置くと危ないものやソファの高さの安全性などを分析できるという。さらに、文字による記録だけでなく、こどもが飲み込んだたばこの吸い殻やボタンなどの現物も保管されている。現場の写真を撮ってもらうこともあるそうだ。これらのデータは、2006年頃から工学系の研究者と協働するようになり、より有効な分析ができるようになった。この点については、第3章の山中さんと西田佳史さん（産業技術総合研究所）の対談を参照されたい。

　このような研究成果をふまえ、山中さんはこどもの事故予防に関する講演を行っている。地域のゲートキーパーでありながら、広く世界に発信する役割を担っている。

The 3 E's to prevent children's accidents and the particular importance of environment

The researcher and educator side of Yamanaka is most apparent in his activities with Safe Kids Japan. This is an NPO established with the goal of preventing injuries to children due to accidents where Yamanaka serves as the chairman. What were the circumstances for starting this?

"When I am on site, I see not only sick children, but also those who come after sustaining injuries and having accidents. For example, there was a 15-month-old child with a burn, and another 6-month-old who had a sticker or something similar lodged in their throat. These everyday accidents are not found in medical textbooks."

There is an approach to preventing these kinds of accidents that involves making changes to the 3 E's, namely environment, education, and enforcement. Among these, "enforcement" takes the longest to change. While "education" is the most frequently conducted element, Yamanaka says that in reality, it does not have much of an effect. What does it not have an effect? According to Yamanaka, "At first, I thought it was because parents were not managing their children well enough, but when I thought about it, I realized it was impossible to keep an eye on a child 24 hours a day. I reconsidered that no matter how careful parents are, things are going to happen." Yamanaka, who felt that there were limits to "enforcement" and "education," focuses on improving the "environment."

The key to improving the environment is collecting information. Yamanaka records detailed accounts of accident scenes. For example, he does not only record "5-year-old, fell down, cut chin." He records the situation in detail: "A 5-year-old was running in the living room and slipped on a rug, cutting his chin on a 50-cm-high wooden armrest on a sofa." In this way, he is able to analyze what things are dangerous to put in the corner of rooms, safe sofa heights, etc. Furthermore, not only does he keep written records, but

国際組織Safe Kids Worldwideの会議にて日本におけるこどもの傷害予防に関する取り組みを紹介する山中さん｜Yamanaka at a Safe Kids Worldwide conference introducing efforts in Japan to prevent children sustaining injuries

山中さんが開発に協力した棚（右）と引き出し（左）。どちらも金具のストッパーがついており、小さなこどもの力では開くことができない　A shelf (right) and chest of drawers (left) that Yamanaka helped develop. Both have metal stoppers that cannot be opened by small children

病気の子も健康な子も安心して利用できる環境

　こどもに優しい環境づくりへの配慮は、クリニックの日々の運営にも及ぶ。緑園こどもクリニックに備え付けられている家具の棚や引き出しは、山中さんが開発に協力したもので、こどもが不用意に開けてしまわないように金具のストッパーが付いている。さらに、予防接種などで来院した健康なこども専用の診察室を設け、クリニックとは出入口も分けている。ここまで徹底して感染管理を行っている事例は少ない。「接点を完全になくすことで、病気の子も健康な子も安心して利用してもらえるようにした」と山中さんは設計の意図を語った。現場に身をおきながら、常に一歩先をみつめて活動している様子がみてとれる。

　最後に、どのような未来をつくりたいか、山中さんに伺った。欧米と比べて、日本の子育て環境には課題があることを指摘したうえで、「日本はこどもの問題を省庁で分断してしまっています。ほかの国では『子ども家庭省』というこどもの問題に特化した省庁があるように、わが国でも省庁が緊密に連携すれば対策が立てやすくなると思います。イギリスには『こどもオンブズマン』というこどもの権利を守るために省庁の上から指揮を執る制度組織があります。日本でもこのような制度組織が必要かもしれません」と語った。保育所は厚生労働省、幼稚園は文部科学省、商業施設は経済産業省、テーマパークは国土交通省というように縦割り行政に翻弄されることの多いわたしたちにとって大変共感する言葉だ。

（仲　綾子）

he retains actual items such as cigarette butts and buttons that children have swallowed. Apparently he sometimes even asks for photographs of the accident site. By working with engineering researchers from around 2006, he has been able to conduct more effective analyses on this data. For more on this, readers should reference the discussion with Yamanaka and Yoshifumi Nishida (National Institute of Advanced Industrial Science and Technology) in Chapter 3.

Based on these research results, Yamanaka holds lectures on preventing children's accidents. In addition to being a community gatekeeper, he also takes on the role of delivering this information to the world at large.

An environment that both sick and healthy children can use with peace of mind

Consideration when creating a child-friendly environment also extends to daily clinic operations. The shelves and drawers that furnish Ryokuen Children's Clinic, which Yamanaka himself helped to develop, include metal stoppers so that children cannot open them carelessly. Furthermore, there is a clinic especially for healthy children who come for things like vaccinations, which even has its own separate entrance. There are not many examples of clinics that take such thorough contagion management measures. Regarding the intent of the clinic's design, Yamanaka said, "By completely eliminating contact, I made it so that both sick and healthy children could use the clinic with peace of mind." Once again, it is clear that Yamanaka is engaging in his activities by constantly thinking one step ahead while putting himself at the scene.

Lastly, I asked Yamanaka what kind of future he wishes to create. He pointed out that Japan's child-raising environment has problems compared to the West in that, "In Japan, children's issues are fragmented into various government ministries and agencies. Other countries have government ministries or agencies that focus specifically on children's problems, such as a "Ministry of Children and Families," and I think if we also worked closely with such a ministry or agency, it would be easier to establish countermeasures. The UK has a system known as the Children's Commissioner which hands down instructions to government agencies in order to protect children's rights. Japan might also need such a system." These are words that we can greatly empathize with in our vertically compartmentalized government where nursery schools are under the jurisdiction of the Ministry of Health, Labour and Welfare, preschools under the Ministry of Education, Culture, Sports, Science and Technology, commercial facilities under the Ministry of Economy, Trade and Industry, and theme parks under the Ministry of Land, Infrastructure, Transport and Tourism.

(Ayako Naka)

▍概要 Summary
緑園こどもクリニック 神奈川県横浜市泉区緑園 2-1-6
Ryokuen Children's Clinic 2-1-6 Ryokuen, Izumi-ku, Yokohama City, Kanagawa
Safe Kids Japan http://safekidsjapan.org/

こどもを育む場が、
地域コミュニティも育む

社会福祉法人あすみ福祉会 茶々保育園グループ

A place that nurtures
children also nurtures the local community

Asumi Social Welfare Society Chacha Nursery School Group

　茶々保育園グループは、1979年に狭山茶の名産地である埼玉県入間市でスタートし、現在は関東近県に14の保育園を運営している。ここは「オトナな保育園」をコンセプトに掲げ、保育園に関わる大人たちはこどもと対等に向き合う。そうすることで、こどもに備わっている能力や感性を伸ばすのだ。保育園を運営する迫田圭子さん・健太郎さんは「こどもに専門家として関わっている保育士の社会的地位を向上したい」と園の役割を情熱的に語る。

　茶々むさしこすぎ保育園にはちゃちゃカフェというセルフサービスのカフェが併設されている。10m^{2}ほどのスペースに8人がけのテーブルが置いてある、スペースの一角にコーヒーメーカーがあり、無料で利用できる。大人向けのインテリアや照明でデザインされた空間には、園児の絵がひとつの作品として飾られている。こどもの絵と軽視せず、その感性を尊重する保育姿勢の表れだ。

　ガラス張りで外に開かれているカフェでは、送り迎えに来た保護者や、保育園のスタッフ、園児が集う。子育ての情報交換もでき、保育園の送り迎えに慣れていないお父さんにとっても、ありがたい居場所になっているようだ。さらには小学生が宿題をしていたり、趣味の俳句を楽しむ初老のご婦人たちが集まったり、コンビニの店員が休憩をしていたり……といった光景もみられ地域の人びとにとっても、かけがえのない、集い、憩う場になっている。

　こどものお迎えに来た保護者と地域のご婦人が自然と会話を交わしているのも印象的だった。保育園が地域の子育ての拠点であると同時に、コミュニケーションの場にもなっている。

　このように、保育園が地域に愛されていると保育園の外でこどもに声をかける大人も増える。ちゃちゃカフェは、こどもを育む保育園が地域コミュニティも育む、という新しい保育園のあり方を提案している。

（松本麻里）

茶々むさしこすぎ保育園にあるちゃちゃカフェの内観
The interior of Chacha Cafe in Chacha Musashikosugi Nursery School ©社会福祉法人あすみ福祉会 茶々保育園グループ／Asumi Social Welfare Society Chacha Nursery School Group

Chacha Nursery School Group was started in 1979 in Iruma City, Saitama, a location famous for Sayama tea (Sayama-cha) . It currently operates 14 nursery centers around the Kanto area. These centers tout the concept of "adult-like nursery school," and adults involved with the nursery school interact with the children on equal terms. This helps to expand on the children's inherent abilities and sensibilities. Keiko and Kentaro Sakoda, who operate the nursery school, speak passionately about its role, saying, "We want to improve the social position of nursery school teachers involved with children as experts."

The Chacha Musashikosugi Nursery School is equipped with a self-service cafe called the Chacha Cafe. The roughly 10m^2 space contains an eight-person table, has a coffee maker in the corner, and is free to use. In this space designed with adult-oriented interior decor and lighting, drawings drawn by the nursery school children are displayed as artwork. This is an expression of a nurturing attitude that does not minimize children's drawings, but respects their sensibilities.

The glass-walled cafe, which is open to the public, is filled with parents who came to drop off or pick up their children as well as nursery school staff and children. This is a place where parents can exchange information on child-raising, and it also seems to be a space that is appreciated by fathers who are not used to picking up and dropping off their children. In addition, I could also see an elementary school student doing homework, middle-aged women enjoying their haiku hobbies, a convenience store employee on break, and others, suggesting that it is also an irreplaceable haven for the people of the community to gather and catch their breaths.

It also left quite an impression to see a guardian who had come to pick up a child naturally exchanging conversation with a local woman. While the nursery school is a center for community child-raising, it is also a place that fosters communication.

If nursery schools are loved like this in their own respective communities, more and more adults will start conversations with children outside of nursery schools. Chacha Cafe sets a new nursery school standard in which a nursery school that nurtures children also nurtures the local community.

(Mari Matsumoto)

授乳・おむつ替えスペース
Nursing and diaper-changing spaces

　子連れでのお出かけに大変さを感じるのは、とりわけ、こどもが小さく、授乳やおむつ替えが必要なときだろう。この時期を過ぎると、目を離すとどこかへ行ってしまうなど別の大変さがともなうものの親の負担感はかなり減る。そこで、ここでは外出時に授乳やおむつ替えができるスペースについて取り上げ、そのデザインについて述べる。

　授乳・おむつ替えスペースの整備は商業施設を中心に進められてきた。2005年頃には居心地の悪く使いにくいものが少なくなかったが、その後、急速に学術研究[1,2,3]や法的整備[4,5]が進み、2018年現在、各施設でさまざまな工夫がなされている。そこでまず、授乳・おむつ替えスペースの整備を先導してきた商業施設から好事例を4つ紹介し、今後の展開について検討する。次に、旅客施設の授乳・おむつ替えスペースの整備プロセスを紹介し、取り組みにあたって重要な考え方を共有する。最後に、これらを総括し、授乳・おむつ替えスペースのデザインについてまとめる。

1. 進化する商業施設の授乳・おむつ替えスペース

　商業施設の授乳・おむつ替えスペースの進化は目覚ましい。ただ、行き過ぎと思われるようなものをみかけることもある。たとえば、お城のような装飾過多なもの、おもちゃなどがそろった至れり尽くせりのものなどだ。このような環境は利用する親子にとって望ましいものだろうか。

　ここでは、今後のあり方を考えるうえで参考になるものとして、4つの事例を紹介したい。はじめの2事例は、こどもと親の行動や気持ちをよく考えたうえで大胆にデザインされた事例といえる。次の2事例は、こどもよりもむしろ親に重点を置いてデザインされた事例だ。いずれも、たんに他の施設と差別化を図って優位性を示すためにデザインするのではなく、授乳やおむつ替えをする親子にとってふさわしい空間はどうあるべきか、という本質的な点から考えてデザインした事例といえる。

■大きな窓から外光が入る明るい空間 —— 二子玉川ライズ・ショッピングセンター
　従来、授乳・おむつ替えスペースはトイレなどに隣接して配置され、窓のない閉鎖的

Perhaps the most difficulty a parent feels when going out with a child occurs when the child is small and needs to be nursed or have his or her diaper changed. Once this stage is over, while there are other difficulties such as the child disappearing somewhere if the parent averts his or her eyes, a parent's feeling of burden greatly decreases. This section will focus on the topic of spaces to nurse and change diapers when going out with children and discuss their design.

The advancement of providing nursing and diaper-changing spaces has centered around commercial facilities. Around 2005, there was no shortage of such spaces that were uncomfortable and hard to use. However, subsequently, academic research[1, 2, 3] and legal provisions[4, 5] advanced quickly, and now, in 2017, many facilities are incorporating a variety of solutions. First, I will introduce four successful cases of commercial facilities that have been leaders in the provision of nursing and diaper-changing spaces and look into their future development. Next, I will introduce the process of installing nursing and diaper-changing spaces in passenger terminal facilities so that we can share important approaches when making such efforts. Finally, I will bring these together and summarize the design of nursing and diaper-changing spaces.

1. The evolution of nursing and diaper-changing spaces at commercial facilities

The evolution of nursing and diaper-changing spaces at commercial facilities is remarkable. However, one often sees those which appear to have been overdone. For example, some are overly decorative, like a castle, and others are piled with toys as if to leave nothing out. Are these types of environments desirable to the children and parents that use them?

Here, I would like to introduce four cases as reference when thinking about the ideal future state. The first two cases can be thought to have been designed boldly after careful consideration for the behavior and feelings of children and parents. The next two were designed with adults in mind more than children. All of these cases look to have

な空間になりがちだったが、二子玉川ライズ・ショッピングセンターのベビールームには大きな窓がある。外光が降り注ぐ、明るく開放的な空間だ。授乳やおむつ替えをするかたわら窓の外の様子を眺めることによって、こどもも大人も気分転換できる。4階に配置されているので、外の道路を行き交う人びとから覗かれる心配もない。

　また、中央には「キリンさんのスペース」と呼ばれる小上がりがあり、抱っこひもやベビーカーからこどもを降ろすことができる。抱っこひもやベビーカーの中に長時間いると、こどもも手足を思い切り伸ばしたくなるだろう。親子ともに一息つくことができる空間が用意されている。親子の行動や気持ちをよく知っているからこそ生まれるデザインだ。

■ 家族みんなが安心して過ごせるゾーン構成 ── セブンパークアリオ柏

　授乳・おむつ替えスペースは、赤ちゃんとママのためだけのものではない。兄弟姉妹やパパをはじめとする家族みんなのためにあるべきだ。このような考え方を実現しているのが、セブンパークアリオ柏の赤ちゃん休憩室だ。ここには、おむつ替え台、授乳ブースに加え、家族が静かに過ごすための年齢別のコーナーがある。

　さらに隣接して、遊具や大型スクリーンを備えたあそび場スカイキッズがある。赤ちゃんとママが授乳やおむつ替えをしている間、兄弟姉妹やパパは所在なく待っているという光景をよくみかけるが、ここでは、兄弟姉妹やパパはスカイキッズであそんでい

セブンパークアリオ柏
SEVEV PARK Ario Kashiwa
右上：乳児、幼児の年齢別にコーナー区画された休憩エリア／左上：授乳室は個室と2〜3名で利用可能なソファーベンチを設置／下：おむつ替えコーナーにはおむつ替え台と併せて体重計、鏡台、家族が待つベンチがある｜Top right: Rest area divided into corners by age / Top left: The nursing room provides individual rooms and a sofa bench that two or three people can use at once / Bottom: In addition to diaper-changing tables, the diaper-changing corner contains a scale, a dressing table, and a bench for families to wait.

二子玉川ライズ・ショッピングセンター
Futako Tamagawa Rise Shopping Center
上：小さなスペースだが、このキリンさんの小上がりが親子の気持ちを緩めてくれる／下：足元からの大きな窓があり外光が差し込む明るい空間。外を眺めて楽しむ親子の姿もみられる｜Top: Despite the small space, this raised "Mr. Giraffe" area helps to relax children and parents / Bottom: A bright space bathed in natural light from the large full height window. Children and parents enjoy looking outside. ©二子玉川ライズ・ショッピングセンター／Futako Tamagawa Rise Shopping Center

been designed from the essential perspective of what an appropriate space should be for children and parents to nurse or change diapers, rather than simply being designed in a way that differentiates them from other facilities in an attempt to exhibit superiority.

■ A bright space that lets in outside light from a large window
—— Futako Tamagawa Rise Shopping Center

In the past, nursing and diaper-changing spaces tended to be adjoined with restrooms and were insular spaces with no windows, but the baby room at Futako Tamagawa Rise Shopping Center has large windows. Natural light pours into the bright, open space. While nursing and changing diapers, both children and adults can look out the window for a change of scenery. It is located on the fourth floor, so there is no worry of being seen by the people passing on the street outside.

In addition, there is a raised area in the center called "Mr. Giraffe's Space" where children can be taken out of their baby carriers or strollers and set down. After spending

ストックホルムのデパート
A Department Store in Stockholm
左：写真中央の木の扉が授乳・おむつ替えスペースの入口／右上：落ち着い
た壁紙と照度を落とした授乳スペース。写真下部の黒いソファに座って授乳
する／右下：手洗いカウンターの一角にシンプルなおむつ替え台（クッショ
ン）を配置している　Left: The wooden door in the center of the photograph is
the entrance to the nursing and diaper-changing space / Top right: The nursing
space with soothing wallpaper and lighting. Mothers sit on the black sofa toward
the bottom of the photograph and nurse / Bottom right: A simple diaper-
changing table (cushion) is placed on one corner of the wash basin counter

られる。赤ちゃん休憩室とスカイキッズの間は動線が短く、見通しもよいため、お互い
に見失うこともなく、家族みんなが安心して過ごすことができる。

■ 大人に目を向けてデザインされた空間 —— ストックホルムのデパート

　次に、授乳・おむつ替えスペースのもうひとつの方向性を示唆する事例としてストッ
クホルムのあるデパートの事例を紹介する。そもそもスウェーデンでは、授乳はどこで
でもできるので特別な部屋はいらないという考え方が一般的だ。ただし、よく探すと小
さな部屋が設けられている場合がある。この部屋にはこども向けのキャラクターなどは
一切なく、落ち着いた色合いで、照度も落としている。大人がリラックスして授乳やお
むつ替えをすることがこどもの心地よさにつながるという考え方を明確に空間として示
している。

■ ホテルのような落ち着いた空間 —— タカシマヤタイムズスクエア〔東京・新宿〕

　大人に目を向けてデザインした事例は、スウェーデンなどの海外に限ったことではな
い。タカシマヤタイムズスクエアのレストランフロアにある赤ちゃん休憩室は、他と一
線を画している。商業施設でよくみかけるカラフルで明るすぎるものとは対照的に、ブ
ラウン、ペールブルー、アイボリーの３色を基調とし、間接照明やブラケットランプ
を用いたホテルのような落ち着いた雰囲気だ。

a long time in a baby carrier or stroller, children are sure to appreciate a good stretch. This space provides a place where children and parents can take a break together. This design would not be possible without thorough knowledge of the behavior and feelings of children and parents.

■ A zone where the whole family can relax —— SEVEN PARK Ario Kashiwa

Nursing and diaper-changing spaces are not only for babies and mothers. They should be for the whole family, from siblings to fathers. This method of thinking has been put into practice at the baby room at SEVEN PARK Ario Kashiwa. Here, in addition to diaper-changing tables and nursing booths, there are also corners separated by age group for the family to wait quietly.

Furthermore, attached to this is the Sky Kids play area furnished with play equipment and a large screen. Fathers and siblings are often seen waiting aimlessly while mothers nurse and change the baby, but here, they can play at Sky Kids. The line of movement between the baby room and Sky Kids is short with a clear line of sight, so the whole family can have a relaxing experience without losing sight of one another.

■ A space designed for adults —— a department store in Stockholm

Next, I will introduce a department store in Stockholm as another suggestion for the

タカシマヤタイムズスクエア（東京・新宿）
Takashimaya Times Square – Shinjuku, Tokyo
左上：フロア全体の環境に馴染む色づかいとシンプルなサイン／右上：おむつ替え中の赤ちゃんの目に直接光源が入らない間接照明／下：手洗い場の鏡面に設置されたシックなブラケット照明 | Top left: Colors that match the environment of the whole floor and a simple design / Top right: Ambient lighting that does not directly enter the eyes of babies on the changing table / Bottom: Chic bracket lighting installed on the mirror surface of the wash basin

これらのほかにも優れた事例はあるが、従来の授乳・おむつ替えスペースにはみられない新しい考え方を示すものとして、以上の4つの事例を紹介した。商業施設の授乳・おむつ替えスペースは、いまや設置されていることがほぼ必須となっており、そのデザインには今後も新たな展開がみられるだろう。ただし、目指すところは、表層的な装飾や過剰なサービスではなく、利用者の行動や心理をよく理解したデザインだ。ここで紹介した事例は、この点で学ぶべきことが多い。

2.新たな試みに挑む旅客施設の授乳・おむつ替えスペース
——JR東日本　子育て中の社員を中心としたワーキンググループ

　移動中の授乳やおむつ替えに困った経験のある人は多いだろう。商業施設と比べて駅などの旅客施設では授乳・おむつ替えスペースはあまり整備されていない。しかし、最近では、とくに新幹線停車駅を中心に新しい試みがみられるようになった。その整備プロセスにはどのような挑戦があったのだろうか。そこには、これまであまり授乳・おむつ替えスペースを積極的に整備してこなかった旅客施設の他の事例や、今後の整備が期待されている公共施設などにとって参考になる取り組み方があるだろうと考え、JR東日本大宮支社にてインタビュー調査を行った。

■設計にママ・パパの声を取り入れる

　インタビュー調査には、本プロジェクトに携わった総勢11名が参加してくれた。そ

インタビュー調査に協力いただいたワーキンググループのメンバー｜Members of the working group who participated in the interview

direction of a nursing and diaper-changing space. In Sweden, it is generally accepted that nursing can be done anywhere, so there is no need for a special room. However, if one looks closely, small rooms are sometimes provided. These rooms do not feature any children's characters — only relaxed colors and soft lighting. This space clearly exhibits the belief that when a parent is able to relax while nursing and changing diapers, that feeling of comfort will be passed on to the children.

■ A relaxed, hotel-like space —— Takashimaya Times Square – Shinjuku, Tokyo
Cases that were designed with adults in mind are not limited to foreign countries such as Sweden. The baby room on the restaurant floor of Takashimaya Times Square is a departure from the rest. In contrast to the bright, colorful baby rooms often found in commercial facilities, this is a relaxed, hotel-like space with ambient lighting and bracket lamps, based on a three-color scheme of brown, pale blue, and ivory.

While there are other excellent cases besides these, these are the four cases I have chosen to introduce as spaces that exhibit a new approach that has not been traditionally seen in nursing and diaper-changing spaces. These days, it is almost mandatory for commercial facilities to provide nursing and diaper-changing spaces, and there are sure to be new developments from here on out. However, the aim should not be a design with superficial decorations and excessive services, but one with a deep understanding of user behaviors and psychologies. There is a lot that we can learn about this from the cases introduced here.

2. New challenges for nursing and diaper-changing spaces at passenger terminal facilities
—— JR East's working group made up mainly of employees who are currently raising children

There are probably many people who have experienced trouble nursing or changing diapers while in transit. Compared to commercial facilities, not many train stations and other passenger terminal facilities are equipped with nursing and diaper-changing spaces. Recently, however, new efforts in this regard can be seen in such facilities, particularly in stations serviced by the Shinkansen bullet train. What challenges are faced during the process of providing these spaces? I went to JR East's Omiya Branch Office to conduct interviews, thinking that I would find efforts that would serve as a reference for other cases of passenger terminal facilities and public facilities that had yet to be proactive in providing nursing and diaper-changing spaces that will be expected to provide them going forward.

■ Incorporating the voices of mothers and fathers for the design
A total of 11 people involved in this project agreed to participate in an interview. Two

待合室の中に設置された授乳室 | A nursing room inside the waiting area

のうち2名は赤ちゃん連れである。つまり、育休中の方がお子さんとともに協力して
くれた。このような姿勢こそが、本プロジェクトの整備プロセスの特徴を示している。
「まずは2008年頃に本社の施策ということでベビー休憩室の整備がはじまりました」
と大宮支社設備部の真保聡裕さんは話しはじめた。JR東日本にはベビー休憩室の基本
的な仕様についてのマニュアルが整備されている。その通りにつくれば無難にベビー休
憩室はできあがる。だが、そこから一歩踏み出す試みがあった。

　2015年3月に子育て中の社員が中心となってワーキンググループを立ち上げ、コン
セプトをつくりはじめたのだ。最初は利用者として「こういうのだったらいいよね」と
いう話からはじめ、SNSなどを利用して授乳やおむつ替えに関わる情報を広く集めた。
ワーキンググループには、ママだけでなく、パパや独身の社員も参加し、幅広い視点を
取り入れて2015年10月に「家族旅行にやさしく、温かみと地域特性が感じられるベ
ビー休憩室」というコンセプトがまとまった。

　JR東日本のような大きな、そして一見かたくみえる組織の中に、このような柔軟な
ワーキンググループが生まれたことは意外に思えるが、その前提として、女性が出産後
に復職しやすい職場環境がきちんと整備されていることがある。このような職場環境な
くして、本プロジェクトは実現しなかっただろう。

■ 小窓がある小山駅のベビー休憩室
　JR東日本では、2016年3月末までに上越、東北、長野新幹線の停車駅21駅21箇
所においてベビー休憩室を整備した（在来線停車駅も含めると48駅53箇所）。そのうちのひ
とつ、小山駅のベビー休憩室を紹介したい。

of them had babies with them. In other words, people on maternity leave participated together with their children. This attitude expresses what is unique about the provision process for this project.

According to Akihiro Shinbo of the Omiya Branch Office Facilities Department, "We first started providing baby rooms around 2008 as a policy from company headquarters." JR East provides a manual on the basic specifications for baby rooms. If it is followed exactly, the installation of baby rooms will go off without a hitch. However, there was an effort to make further strides from this.

In March 2015, a working group was formed mostly of employees who were currently raising children, and the group began to create a concept. The group first began by discussing what kind of space they would like to make use of as users. It then used social media and similar platforms to collect a variety of information related to nursing and diaper-changing. The working group was composed not only of mothers, but also fathers and single employees, and thus incorporated a wide range of viewpoints. In October 2015, it was decided that the concept would be "a baby room that is family trip-friendly and exudes warmth and local flavor."

It may be surprising that such a flexible working group was formed at an organization

右上：E5系新幹線の運転席が描かれたキッズスペースの小窓／左上：小窓はコンコースに面している／左下：壁に電車が描かれたおむつ替えスペース　Top right: A small window in the kid's space that features a drawing of the driver's seat of an E5 Shinkansen / Top left: The window gives a view of the concourse / Bottom left: One of the walls in the diaper changing space features a drawing of a train

待合室の一角に設置されたベビー休憩室には、授乳スペースとおむつ替えスペースとキッズスペースが設けられており、キッズスペースの壁の一部に小窓が開けられ、室内外ともにE5系新幹線の運転席が描かれている。室内にいるこどもは小窓を通してコンコースの様子を眺めることができ、通勤などでコンコースを利用する人もベビー休憩室の存在を知ることができる。小窓は両者をつなぐ役割を果たしている。

■ こどもの環境を考えることは、新たな地平を切り開くこと

　インタビュー調査に協力いただいた11名全員に本プロジェクトを通して思うところを語っていただいた。すべてを紹介することはできないが、とりわけ印象に残った言葉をいくつか共有したい。

　ベビー休憩室の整備を統括した中人美香さんは、「小さいこどもを連れて電車に乗れる。電車に乗ったらそこでおばあちゃんとか同世代のママとかに会ってお話できる。家に閉じこもっているよりも電車のなかで世界が広がる。そういうふうに、みんなが気軽に外出できる環境を整えて一緒に外に出ていきたいなと思います」と語ってくれた。話し終えた瞬間に、生後4カ月（取材当時）のお子さんがママのお膝のうえで「あー」と声をだした。まるで「賛成！」と言っているかのように。利用者のために整備をしてあげるという姿勢ではなく、一緒に出ていきたいという言葉にママとしての優しいまなざしが伺える。

　また、整備担当の佐藤景子さんも赤ちゃんを抱きながら「いままでなんでも自分ひとりでがんばってきたように思っていて、まわりとの関わりを意識していなかった。こどもが生まれてから、まわりに支えられている、地域に生かされていると感謝するようになった」と語った。ワーキンググループでの活動は、要望を声高に叫ぶものではなく、自らの足元をみつめて感謝することにつながったようだ。

　最後に、営業部の松村亮典さんは「新しいことをしたいと思っている」とつぶやいた。こどものための空間をつくりだすことは、こどもに媚びたデザインをすることではなく、新たな地平を切り開くことだという表明に共感する人は多いだろう。

インタビューに答えるプロジェクトメンバー｜Project members who participated in the interview

as large and seemingly rigid as JR East, but it was preceded by a workplace environment in which there is a firmly established system whereby women can easily return to work after maternity leave. Without such a workplace environment, this project would probably not have been possible.

■ A baby room with a small window at Oyama Station

By the end of March 2016, JR East had baby rooms installed in 21 locations in 21 stations on the Joetsu, Tohoku, and Nagano Shinkansen lines (53 locations in 48 stations if local line stations are included). One of those, which I would like to introduce, is the baby room at Oyama Station.

In the baby room, which is located in the corner of the waiting area, a nursing and diaper-changing space are provided along with a kid's space. On one part of the wall of the kid's space, there is a small window with a drawing of the driver's seat on an E5 Series Shinkansen on both the inside and outside of the room. Children inside the room can look out at the concourse through the small window, and those using the concourse to commute to work or other reasons can also see that there is a baby room. The small window fills the role of connecting both sides.

■ Considering children's environments means breaking new ground

The 11 people who participated in the interview shared their thoughts throughout the project. I cannot introduce all of them, but I would like to share several answers that left a particularly strong impression.

Mika Nakahito, who supervised the installation of the baby rooms, said, "I want an environment where people can smoothly ride the train with small children. Where you can meet and talk with grandmothers and same-generation mothers on the train. Where, rather than being locked up in the house, our worlds would expand aboard the train. I want to provide an environment like that, where everyone could go out together, and

インタビューを終え、JR東日本大宮支社を後にするとき、「安全とは命を守ること」という看板が目に入った。インタビューの最中にも「安全」という言葉を何度となく耳にした。このような方針を掲げるJR東日本は、実はこどもの空間づくりにとても親和性が高いのではないだろうか。なぜなら、こどもの空間づくりにおいて安全性は最も大切なことのひとつだから。

3. 授乳・おむつ替えスペースのデザイン

　これまで、商業施設と旅客施設の授乳・おむつ替えスペースのデザインと整備プロセスについてみてきた。商業施設では、大人にも目を向けてデザインすることの重要性を学んだ。旅客施設では、ママ、パパとしての自分の経験に加え、他者の経験を設計プロセスに取り込むことの展開可能性を知った。実は、これらは、第1章で述べた「こどもも大人も心地よい空間」をデザインする7つの指針に重なる。つまり、「こどもも大人も主役」ということと、「他者の経験に学ぶ」ということだ。

　インタビュー調査をはじめた当初は、こどもが小さい時期は特別な配慮が必要だろうと考え、授乳・おむつ替えスペースに着目した。しかし、わたしたちがたどりついたひとつの答えは、授乳やおむつ替えを必要とする赤ちゃんを対象とした空間であっても、デザインにおいて大切にすべき点は、第1章で示した7つの指針「主役、専門性、経験、本物、きっかけ、調整、継続」から外れるものではないということだ。これらは、こどもの年齢を問わず、「こどもも大人も心地よい空間」をデザインするうえで有効な考え方といえるだろう。

　なお、授乳・おむつ替えスペースの具体的な設計指針として、筆者らはベビー休憩室コンセプトブック[※6]を策定した。概要を以下にまとめるが、詳しくは本コンセプトブックをご参照いただきたい。

■授乳・おむつ替えスペースの設計ポイント
1. 配置
①見つけやすく、わかりやすい場所、②不審者が立ち入らないような人目の多い場所、③一箇所に集中配置するのではなく、複数箇所に分散配置することが望ましい。
2. 規模
①赤ちゃん連れが多く利用する施設では50㎡以上、②赤ちゃん連れが利用することもある施設では30㎡程度、③最小単位として、授乳のみを行う室の広さは2～3㎡、授乳とおむつ替えを行う室の広さは5～6㎡を目安とする。
3. ゾーニング
①授乳ゾーンとおむつ替えゾーンを分離する、②緩衝帯を設け、休憩・情報発信ゾーン等とする、③個室授乳ブースと共用授乳コーナーを併設する。
4. 動線
①授乳ゾーンとおむつ替えゾーンの動線を交錯させない、②ベビーカー置き場を確保

I want to go out with everyone." As soon as she finished speaking, a 4-month-old (at the time of the interview) sitting on her lap exclaimed "Ah!" as if to say, "I agree!" When she said that she wanted to go out with everyone, rather than the attitude of providing something for users, I saw the kind gaze of a mother.

Furthermore, Keiko Sato, in charge of installation, said while holding a baby, "It feels like I have worked hard to do everything myself thus far, without being conscious of my relationship with those around me. Ever since I had a baby, I started to feel grateful for the support from those around me and encouragement from the community." The working group's activities have led to not merely shouting out demands, but looking at their own situations and being grateful.

Lastly, Ryosuke Matsumoto of the Sales Department murmured, "We want to do something new." Many people would probably agree that creating a space for children means not creating a design that panders to children, but breaking new ground.

After the interviews, when I was leaving JR East's Omiya Branch Office, a sign caught my eye that said "Safety means protecting lives." The word "safety" had also come up many times during the interviews. With such a policy, perhaps JR East is indeed highly compatible with the creation of spaces for children. After all, safety is one of the most important factors when creating spaces for children.

3. Designing nursing and diaper-changing spaces

Thus far, we have examined the design and provision process for nursing and diaper-changing spaces in commercial facilities and passenger terminal facilities. In commercial facilities, we learned the importance of designing such spaces with adults in mind. In passenger terminal facilities, we learned about development that can occur when including the experiences of others in the provision process in addition to personal experiences as mothers and fathers. These actually overlap with the seven guidelines for designing "spaces that are comfortable for both children and adults" listed in Chapter 1. In the first case we found the importance of "giving both children and adults the lead roles," and in the second case, "learning from the experiences of others."

When we initially began the interviews, we focused on nursing and diaper-changing spaces because we thought that children probably need special consideration when they are small. However, the one answer that we arrived at was, even if a space is geared towards babies who need nursing and diaper-changing, the most important aspects during the design stage do not stray far from the seven guidelines listed in Chapter 1: "lead role, expertise, experience, the 'real thing,' opportunities, adjustments, and continuity." These can be considered effective approaches when designing a "space that is comfortable for both children and adults," regardless of the age of the child.

Incidentally, we have drafted a baby room concept book[6] to serve as specific design guidelines for nursing and diaper-changing spaces. These guidelines are summarized

する、③ 男性も利用する動線と女性のみが利用する動線を明示する。

5. インテリアデザイン

① リラックスできるしつらえ、② 動くものを目で追う等の赤ちゃんの心理や行動特性をふまえたしつらえ、③ 男性も気軽に入れるしつらえとする。

6. 照明

① 光源が目に直接入らない間接照明、② コーブ照明（器具を上向きに設置して天井面に反射させる）、③ Ra（平均演色評価数）80 以上の肌の色が自然に見える照明とする。

7. 設備

① 手洗器とシンクを個別に設置する、② おむつ用ゴミ箱を設置する、③ 飲料の自動販売機やウォーターサーバなどの設置を検討する。

8. 細やかな心くばり

① 荷物置きやコート掛けを設置する、② 兄弟姉妹のための家具等を設置する、③ BGM、アロマなども利用者の満足度向上を図る有効な手段となる。

（仲 綾子、西本 彩）

―――

※1 田才知未、森傑：「男女共同参画からみた親子休憩室の実態と課題－札幌市内における商業施設を対象として－」日本建築学会計画系論文集 第76巻 第666号、pp.1379-1388、2011 ｜ Tasai, T. and Mori, S. "Actual Conditions and Issues on the Family Room for Baby Care from the Viewpoint of Gender Equality: Based on the Survey of Commercial Facilities in Sapporo." Journal of Architecture and Planning (Transactions of AIJ) Vol. 666 (pp.1379-1388) , 2011.

※2 仲綾子、内田将夫：「ベビー休憩室コンセプトブックの開発と評価」日本建築学会技術報告集 第49号、pp.1173-1176、2015 ｜ Naka, A. and Uchida, M. "Development and Evaluation of Baby Room Concept Book" AIJ Journal of Technology and Design Vol. 49 (pp.1173-1176) 2015.

※3 仲綾子、谷口新：「複合商業施設における行動観察調査にもとづくおむつ替えゾーンを中心としたベビー休憩室の利用実態と計画課題」日本建築学会計画系論文集第724号、pp.1,259-1,268、2016 ｜ Naka, A. and Taniguchi, S. "User Behavior and Planning Issues Focused on Diaper Changing Zones in Baby Rooms in Commercial Complex Facilities Based on the Observation Surveys" Journal of Architecture and Planning (Transactions of AIJ) Vol. 724 (pp.1,259-1,268) , 2016.

※4 国土交通省：「高齢者、障害者等の円滑な移動等に配慮した建築設計標準」2.13F.1、pp.2-136～2-139、2007（2012、2017改訂）｜ Ministry of Land, Infrastructure, Transport and Tourism (MLIT) . "Construction and Design Standards for the Smooth Transportation, etc. of Elderly Persons, Disabled Persons, etc." 2.13F.1 (pp.2-136 - 2-139) , 2007 (revised in 2012 and 2017) .

※5 東京都：「高齢者、障害者等が利用しやすい建築物の整備に関する条例（建築物バリアフリー条例）」第10条二項ハおよび別表第三、2006 ｜ Tokyo Metropolitan Government. "Ordinance for the Development of Buildings Accessible to Elderly Persons, Disabled Persons, etc. (Barrier-free Building Ordinance) ." (Article 10, Paragraph 2-3 and Appendix 3) , 2006.

※6 コンビウィズ株式会社　編集・発行：『ベビー休憩室コンセプトブック』、2013（自社製品の宣伝は記載せず、ベビー休憩室の計画・設計に有用な情報を公共知として無償で提供している）。｜ CombiWith Corporation (editor/publisher) . "Baby Room Concept Book, 2013." (This book provides, as public knowledge, free information that is useful in the planning and design of baby rooms, with no advertisements for its own products.)

below, but the concept book itself can be referenced for further details.

■ Key points for designing nursing and diaper-changing spaces

1. Location

They should be located in ①an accessible location, ②a prominent, public area to hinder the entry of suspicious people, and ③dispersed over multiple locations rather than concentrated in one area.

2. Size

The following measurements should be used: ①At least 50 m² for facilities frequently used by people with babies, ②roughly 30 m² for facilities occasionally used by people with babies, and ③a minimum of 2 to 3 m² for a dedicated nursing room and 5 to 6 m² for a room that will be used for both nursing and diaper-changing.

3. Zoning

①The nursing zone and the diaper-changing zone should be separated, ②buffer zones should be provided and the space used as a rest zone, information communication zone, etc., ③both individual nursing booths and a communal nursing corner should be provided.

4. Line of movement

①The movement lines for the nursing zone and the diaper-changing zones should not be allowed to cross, ②there should be space to park strollers, ③it should be clearly indicated which lines of movement men can use and which are only for women.

5. Interior design

The design should ①be relaxing, ②take into account the psychology and behavioral traits of babies, for example, that they follow any moving object with their eyes, and ③be welcoming for men as well.

6. Lighting

The lighting should be ①ambient lighting where the source of light does not directly enter the eyes, ②cove lighting (in which the equipment is installed facing upwards and reflects off of the ceiling), ③at least Ra 80 on the general color rendering index so that skin tone appears natural.

7. Facilities

The following facilities should be considered: ①a separate wash basin and sink, ②a dedicated trash can for diapers, ③a vending machine for drinks and/or a water server.

8. Detailed considerations:

Effective ways to improve the level of user satisfaction include ①baggage racks and coat hooks, ②furniture, etc. for siblings, ③background music, aromas, etc.

(Ayako Naka, Aya Nishimoto)

こどもと過ごす空間づくりを考える
Thinking about creating spaces that are comfortable for children

本章では、こどもと過ごす空間づくりに役立つ情報として以下の3項目について解説する。各項目とも一目でわかりやすく伝わるようにイラストを用いて解説しているので、実際にデザインの仕事に関わらない方々にも気軽に楽しんで読んでもらいたい。

1. こどもあるある（こどもの謎の行動）

こどもは、大人とは異なる特有の行動特性をもつ。たとえば、むやみに走りまわる、隙間にはさまるなど、さまざまな行動が挙げられる。これらを把握しておくことは、安全を検討するうえで有効だろう。さらに、想定外のこどもの行動から新しいデザインのアイデアが生まれる可能性もあるだろう。

2. 安全

こどもの空間において、安全への配慮は重要だ。あらゆる事故を防止すべく、いわば"過保護"な空間とする必要はないが、重大な事故を引き起こす可能性がある空間構成やディテールは避けたい。ここでは、具体的な安全策（台の高さ、手すり子の間隔など）を提示するよりも、よく起きる事故の状況を提示するほうがデザインする際に工夫しやすいと考え、こどもの行動から引き起こされる事故事例を示している。

なお、安全については、国土交通省による指針[1]に記載されているリスクとハザードの考え方が参考になる。端的に言えば、危険性をこどもが判断できるリスクと判断できないハザードに区分し、リスクを適切に管理し、ハザードは除去することを基本とするものだ。さらに、商業施設の安全については、経済産業省によるガイドライン[2]に基本的な考え方をとりまとめているので、関心のある方はご参照いただきたい。

3. 空間デザイン

こどもも大人もともに心地よく過ごす空間にはどのようなデザインが求められるだろうか。わたしたちがこれまで行ったインタビュー調査の結果をふまえ、スケール、色彩、明るさ／照明、素材、アイテムなどについて説明する。

いずれの項目も、すべての事象を網羅しているわけではない。紙面の都合上、わたしたちが収集した事例のなかから、起こる可能性が高いものや重要度が高いものを選んで掲載している。ここで挙げた事例は一部にすぎないが、これをきっかけに議論が深まることを願っている。

（仲 綾子）

---

[1] 国土交通省：「都市公園における遊具の安全確保に関する指針（改訂第2版）」、2014年6月
Ministry of Land, Infrastructure, Transportation and Tourism. "Guideline for Ensuring the Safety of Playground Equipment in City Parks (Ver. 2)." June 2014.

[2] 経済産業省：「商業施設内の遊戯施設の安全に関するガイドライン（Ver.1.0）」、2016年6月
Ministry of Economy, Trade and Industry. "Guidelines for Safe Use of Play Facilities on the Premises of Commercial Facilities (Ver. 1.0)." June 2016.

This chapter will comment on the following three informational items that are useful when creating spaces for children. Each is explained with illustrations to make them clearer and immediately understandable. It is our hope that people who are not actually involved in design work will also casually enjoy reading it.

1. Common occurrences with children (the puzzling behavior of children)

Children have unique behavioral traits that differ from adults. For example, I could list several behaviors such as running around at random, getting stuck in small spaces, etc. Understanding these is sure to be useful when considering safety. Furthermore, children's unexpected behaviors are sure to lead to new design ideas.

2. Safety

In children's spaces, consideration for safety is essential. While there is no need for a so-called "overprotected" space that prevents any kind of accident, it is important to avoid spatial structures and detailing that may lead to a major accident. Rather than presenting specific safety measures (table height, intervals between banisters, etc.) , I have determined that listing frequently-occurring accidents will make it easier to solve these issues during the design stage. As such, this chapter will present cases of accidents that have occurred due to the behavior of children.

The basis of safety is the adequate management of risks and removal of hazards as described in guidelines published by the Ministry of Land, Infrastructure, Transport and Tourism[1]. Furthermore, the basic concept regarding safety in commercial facilities is summarized in guidelines published by the Ministry of Economy, Trade and Industry[2], so I encourage those interested to refer to these documents.

3. Spatial design

What kind of design is required in a space that is comfortable for both children and adults? This section will explain scale, colors, brightness/lighting, materials, objects, etc. based on the results of the interviews that we conducted.

None of these items necessarily covers all cases. Due to space restrictions, we have chosen several cases from those we gathered that were most likely to occur and had the highest level of importance. The cases given here are only a small portion of the whole, but we hope they will help to deepen the discussion. (Ayako Naka)

1 こどもあるある（こどもの謎の行動）
Common occurrences with children（the puzzling behavior of children）

誰もが「あるある！」と思い当たるような、こどもに特有の行動がある。なぜか
こどもはやりたがるが、大人になるとあまりやらない。このような行動を「こど
もあるある」と名づけて、以下に集めた。

Children have certain unique behaviors that anyone would make almost anyone say, "That's
so true!" For some reason, children tend to do certain things that adults rarely do. Some of
these "common occurrences with children" are listed below.

よーい どん！
Ready, set, go!

走る
Running

むやみに走り回る。広い空間に出る
と急に走り出したくなったり、くねくね
と蛇行したくなったりする。

Running around at random. When they enter
a large space, children want to run or zig-zag
through it.

空想する
Using their imaginations

「青いタイルは海でサメがいるから白い
タイルのところだけ歩く」など、自分のい
る現実の場所を別の空間に見立てる。

They turn the place where they actually are into
somewhere completely different. For example,
"The blue tiles are the ocean, and there are
sharks in there, so I'll only walk on the white
tiles."

白いところだけ歩こう！
I'll only walk
on the white tiles!

跳ねる
Jumping

高いところから飛び降りる、水たまりに飛び込む、うれしくて思わずその場で飛び上がる。こどもはなにかと跳ねる。

Children will jump from a high place, jump into a puddle, and suddenly jump for joy when they are happy. They will jump for any reason.

それっ！
Here I go!

大きさ、同じかな?!
Are mine the same size?

はめる／重ねる
Filling/overlapping

地面に書かれた標識の足のマークの上に自分の足を重ねるなど、大人が記号として捉えるものも見逃さない。

Children do not miss things that serve as symbols for adults, such as putting their own feet on top of signs that show foot marks on the ground.

ぴったり入った！
I fit!

はさまる
Entering small spaces

ダンボールの箱、壁と家具の隙間、ベッドの下など、身体を入れられそうなスペースをみつけると、はさまりに行く。

When children find somewhere they might be able to fit, whether it be a cardboard box, the gap between the wall and a piece of furniture, or under the bed, they will get inside it.

口に入れる
Putting things in their mouths

とくに乳幼児期には、唇や舌でものを確かめるかのように、なんでも口に入れる。飲み込んでしまうこともある。

Especially during infancy, children put everything into their mouths as if to check things out with their lips and tongues. Occasionally, they accidentally swallow things.

あむ あむ
Num, num!

みてみてー！
"Look, look!

のぼる
Climbing

歩道の縁石、花壇のへりなど、一段上がったところにのぼりたがる。連続したところだと、その上をずっと歩く。

Children like to climb up to higher places like the raised curb of a sidewalk or the edge of a flower bed. If the raised portion continues, they will walk on top of it the whole time.

落とす
Dropping things

わざと落とす。落ち方を眺めたり、落とした先をじっと見つめたりする。何度も繰り返して落とすことも多い。

Children drop things on purpose. They watch the way it falls and stare at where it fell. They often keep dropping the item over and over.

ポイ
ポイ
Plop!
Plop!

触る
Touching

とにかく触りたがる。汚いものでも触る。手すりなど連続しているものは、ずっと触り続ける。

Children like to touch things. They will even touch dirty things. They will continuously keep their hands on things that continue like railings.

集める
Gathering

やたらとものを集める。どんぐり、落ち葉、花といった自然なものから、たばこの吸い殻のような汚いものまで。

Children gather things profusely. From object in nature like acorns, leaves, and flowers, to dirty things like cigarette butts.

2 安全

こどもの行動から引き起こされる典型的な事故の状況を以下にまとめた。安全な空間をつくりだすための手がかりとして活用してもらいたい。

Below is a list of typical accident situations caused by children's behavior. Please use this as a guide to create safe spaces.

見失った！
I can't find my child!

こどもは隙間などに入りたがるので、見失ってしまうことがある。こどもの身体寸法と空間の寸法との関係を把握しておこう。

Since children like to go into small spaces, parents sometimes lose sight of them. Gain an understanding of the relationship between the body measurements of children and the size of the space.

抜けなくなった！
My child can't get out!

身体の部分のうち、とくに頭は入れられても出せないことがある。こどもの身体の各部分のサイズを理解しておこう。

Out of all body parts, children tend to get their heads stuck in things the most. Know the size of each part of a child's body.

転んだ！
My child tripped!

こどもが転ぶことは、もはや起こることを前提として捉えたい。転んだあとのこと、床の硬さや家具の納まりに注意しよう。

It should be considered a given that children will trip. Consider what should be done after they fall, the hardness of floors, and the location of furniture.

イタッ！
Ouch!

あっ
Uh oh!

イタッ！
Ouch!

落ちた！
My child fell!

のぼりたがり、跳ねたがるこどもは落ちることも多い。「転んだ！」と同様に、落ちたあとのことを検討しよう。

Children who like to climb and jump often fall. Just as with tripping, consider what will happen after the fall.

指を挟んだ！
My child's finger got pinched!

好奇心からわざと指を差し入れたり、不注意で指を挟んだり。大けがにならないよう工夫しよう。

Out of curiosity, children will purposely put their fingers in things and wind up getting them pinched. Devise ways to avoid major injuries.

あっ
Aggh!

イタッ！
Ouch!

こどもの事故予防に、
空間づくりとテクノロジーの観点を

山中龍宏さん（緑園こどもクリニック院長）✕
西田佳史さん（産業技術総合研究所首席研究員）

Tatsuhiro Yamanaka

Yoshifumi Nishida

こどもが過ごす空間づくりでは、危険をなくすことが最重要項目。施設の運営側にはどのような配慮が求められるのか。こどもの事故予防に取り組む小児科医の山中龍宏さんと、産業技術総合研究所の西田佳史さんに対談していただいた。

―― お二人がこどもの傷害予防に取り組むきっかけは何だったのでしょうか？

山中 病院で診療をしていると、病気だけでなく怪我をしたこどもも毎日やって来ます。しかも、同じ事故が同じような年齢層の間で起きている。また、新しい製品が出まわると必ず新しい事故が起きます。昔、シュレッダーが登場したときに、こどもが指を入れて指が切れる事故が何件も発生しました。予防するには、シュレッダーの口にこどもの指が入らない、あるいは入っても指先が刃に到達しない設計をすればいい。いまはこれに関しては改善がなされています。しかし、日本には製品化される以前の予防措置がうまくできていない事例がまだまだあります。

　親は、「私が見ていなかったから」と自分を責めて終わりにしてしまい、事故の情報はどこにも伝えられません。重症度が高い事故が受診する医療現場で情報を取り、専門家に伝える必要があると思います。

　私は最初、こどもの事故データの収集をひとりでやっていたのですが小児科医だけでは解決できないことがほとんどで、2003年から産総研（産業技術総合研究所）と連携するようになり、初めて情報を活かした解決までたどり着けるようになりました。

西田 僕はロボット工学やセンサーネットワーク（IoTで使用されるネットワーク）が専門分野です。自分にもこどもが生まれたのをきっかけに、こどもの事故について調べたところ山中先生のホームページが出てきて、病院に伺ったのがはじまりです。

　山中先生との連携がはじまって、2005年に「事故サーベイランスプロジェクト」という研究会を立ち上げました。公園遊具について取り上げ、実際にあった事故をもとにケーススタディをし、危険を減らす遊具をメーカーと開発しました。そのときに病院を定点として情報を集め、分析し、工学、メーカーに循環させる社会的なしくみをつくらなければいけないことがみえてきました。当時の日本には、まだそういうしくみがなかったんです。

―― こどもの傷害予防をテーマとした団体NPO法人 Safe Kids Japan の活動についてお聞かせください。

山中 約10年前から成育医療研究センターから事故の情報をもらうようになりました。それを中心にソリューションを考え、いろいろ取り組んできました。なかには法律

The role of spatial creation and technology in preventing child-related accidents

Tatsuhiro Yamanaka (Director of Ryokuen Children's Clinic) ╳
Yoshifumi Nishida (Prime Senior Researcher at the National Institute of Advanced Industrial Science and Technology)

When creating spaces for children, eliminating danger is of the utmost importance. What considerations are expected from the facility management side? I sat down with Tatsuhiro Yamanaka, a pediatrician working to prevent accidents involving children, and Yoshifumi Nishida from the National Institute of Advanced Industrial Science and Technology (AIST).

—— How did you both become involved with children's accident prevention?

Yamanaka : Every day at my clinic, I would see not only sick children, but also those with injuries. Moreover, the same accidents were occurring in the same age groups. Furthermore, when new products would appear on the market, there were sure to be new accidents. Many years ago, when shredders first came out, I saw many cases of children putting their fingers in them and cutting their fingers. In order to prevent this, shredders needed to be designed so that children's fingers could not fit inside, or even if they could fit inside, they should not be able to reach the blades. Now, they have been improved in this regard. However, Japan still has many areas in which preventative measures have not developed well before commercialization.

Parents blame themselves, saying, "I wasn't watching them," and it ends there—information on the accident is not reported to anyone. I think that information on high-severity accidents needs to be recorded by the medical site consulted and reported to experts.

At first, I was gathering the data on children's accidents by myself, but I was unable to resolve most cases with only pediatrics. In 2003, I partnered with the National Institute of Advanced Industrial Science and Technology (AIST), and for the first time, I was able to use this data to reach resolutions.

左：産総研リビングラボのベランダ での事故検証／右：産総研リビング ラボでの遊具で遊ぶこどもの行動 計測 ｜ Left: An accident test on the balcony of AIST's Living Lab / Right: Behavior measurement of children playing with toys in AIST's Living Lab

Nishida : My area of specialty is robotics engineering and sensor networks (networks used in the IoT). When I had a child myself, I researched children's accidents, came across Dr. Yamanaka's website, and paid him a visit.

I began a partnership with Dr. Yamanaka, and in 2005, we launched a workshop called the "Accident Surveillance Project." We focused on the subject of

産総研リビングラボ全景。実生活環境を想定した仮想実験空間 | A complete view of AIST's Living Lab. A virtual experiment space that imagines an actual living environment

の基準の改定につながった例もあります。

　こどもの事故は次から次へと起きます。われわれとしては重症度の高いものからとにかく取り組もうと。まずは医療系が窓口となって情報を集め、その後の分析は工学系に任せます。これら製品や環境の改善と同時に、事故の実態を保護者に知らせ、安全に対する意識を高める活動も必要です。この啓発活動を担っているのが NPO Safe Kids Japan です。

西田　われわれの専門はテクノロジーなので、事故を個人のせいにせず、いかに製品や空間の問題として扱えるかが重要です。最近だとセンサ技術も発達しているので、新たな見守りの技術を開発することも現実味を帯びてきています。事故のような古くからある問題に対して、時代に合わせて解き方を変えていくのが技術者としての役割だと思っています。

—— 空間のプランニングやデザインなど、こどもが過ごす場をつくる人に伝えたいこと、あるいは連携できることがありましたら、お教えください。

山中　そうしたクリエイティブな人なら、データや配慮するべき点を伝えれば、いろいろな解決策を考え出せるのではないでしょうか。

　たとえばベッドが窓の下に設置してある部屋は、こどもがベッドに登って窓から落ちる典型的な事故のパターンなのですが、そのように設置してある部屋の写真をインテリアデザインの宣伝の写真として配布しているものもあります。安全にも着目してデザインする、そういう思考があると、もう一歩進んだデザインになると思います。

西田　集客施設のキッズコーナーなどでは、センサを置いて、そこにあるものがこどもにどのように使われているかを観察し、理解したうえで改善していくのも、今ならできる新しいものづくりの方法だと思います。車の自動ブレーキシステムのように、危ない状況をみつけられるモニタの設置なども十分に狙える技術だと思っています。

—— 活動を通じて以前より変化していると感じること、あるいはしていないと感じることはありますか。

山中　安全に対する社会の関心は高まりつつあるように感じます。しかし、全体のシステムを変えるのはまだ難しいですね。製品関係で言えば、キッズデザイン協議会（こどもたちの安全・安心に貢献するデザインを推奨するNPO団体）ができて、こどもにとって安全な

playground equipment in parks, did case studies based on accidents that actually occurred, and worked with manufacturers to develop less dangerous playground equipment. It was then that we discovered the need to collect information from hospitals, analyze it, and create a social scheme that would allow it to circulate among engineers and manufacturers. There was no such scheme in Japan at the time.

—— Please tell me about the activities of the NPO, Safe Kids Japan, an organization centered on the theme of children's accident prevention.

Yamanaka : About 10 years ago, I started receiving accident information from the National Center for Child Health and Development. I would think of solutions based on that information and I have implemented various efforts. Some of these cases even led to the revision of legal standards.

Children's accidents keep occurring one after the other. We decided to go ahead and start with the most severe cases. I started by gathered information from those in the medical field and left its subsequent analysis to the engineers. Along with improving these products and the environment, it is also necessary to conduct activities to inform guardians of the reality of accidents and increase their awareness of safety. Safe Kids Japan, an NPO, is taking on these enlightenment activities.

Nishida : Our specialty is technology, so it is important to see to what extent we can treat accidents as problems with products and space, rather than blaming them on people. Thanks to recent advances in sensor technology, the development of new protective technology is that much closer to reality. I think that it is our job as engineers to change how age-old problems like accidents are solved in line with the times.

—— What would you like to convey to people involved in spatial planning, design, or other aspects of creating spaces where children spend time? Are there any ways you can collaborate?

Yamanaka : I'm sure that those kinds of creative people could come up with a variety of solutions if we share data and points that should be taken into consideration.

For example, in rooms where the bed is placed under a window, it is a typical accident pattern for children to climb onto the bed and fall out of the window, but photographs of rooms set up this way are distributed as advertisements for interior design. If they have ideas for designs that focus on safety as well, I think it will take the design one step further.

Nishida : I think that putting sensors in kid's corners and similar areas in customer-attracting facilities, monitoring how the children use what is there, and using that understanding to make improvements is a new manufacturing method that is now possible. I think that the installation of monitors that can spot dangerous situations, like automatic braking systems on vehicles, is technology that is entirely possible.

—— Is there anything that you feel has changed, or not changed, because of your activities?

Yamanaka : I feel that society's interest in safety is increasing. However, it is still difficult to change entire systems. With relation to products, the Kids Design Association (an NPO that promotes designs that contribute to children's safety and security) was formed, leading to the development of items that are safe for children and making them easier to obtain.

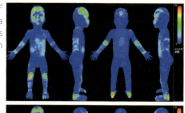

こどもの事故による外傷の受傷分布を示す分析データ。下が安全基準の改善後 | Analytical data that shows the distribution of external injuries sustained by children due to accidents. The bottom data is after revision of the safety standards

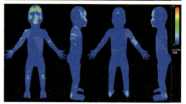

ものが開発され手に入りやすくなってきてきます。

西田　公園の遊具は、2008年と2014年に国交省の基準が見直されて、安全性が高まってきています。しかし学校関係、商業施設の対策はまだまだ対策が十分ではありません。これから取り組むべき課題だと思います。

—— 今後、試したいことはありますか。

西田　人工知能による見守りのシステムはとても高いレベルになってきているので、日常的な暮らしのなかで手つかずだった、ベランダからの転落、風呂場の溺死の対策として新しい方法ができそうだと考えています。親がこどもから目を離す瞬間は誰にでも必ずあるので、今後の方向としては、人だけで見守るのではなく、家にカメラ、センサを付けて人と人工知能のハイブリットで見守るのが理想だと考えています。集客施設、公園でもできたらいいですね。

山中　日本小児科学会のホームページの傷害速報の欄に、われわれ小児科医が現場で経験した事例を掲載しています。この欄は誰でもみることができます。非常にわかりやすく、いろいろな基準の改定にもつながっているので、これをもっと広めたいですね。現在は小児科だけでやっていますが、他科も含め医療界全体で記録・発信をすれば、毎日、何百例も集まると思います。それを人工知能で分析し、予防に役立つデータベースにする必要があると思っています。

　約3年前に、「Safe Kids Japan」というNPO団体を立ち上げ、保護者に対する教育、啓発活動も始めました。こどもの事故は月齢によってどんな事故が起きやすいかが決まっているので、事前に情報提供しやすい。たとえば、誤飲は生後6カ月になったら必ず起こるので、その時期にスマートフォンを通じて注意喚起をするといったシステムも、通信手段が発達したいまの時代なら、できる可能性が高い。効果のある啓発活動をしていきたいですね。

まとめ

こどもの事故を、人の見守りだけで防ぐには限界がある。事故予防には、空間づくりの工夫と科学技術を取り入れる必要がある。とくに空間のデザインは、美観だけの世界観を追求するだけでなく、多様な人に対する安全への配慮がなければいけない。さらに空間ができあがってからも、そこがどのように利用されているか把握し、空間や運営方法を常に改善、進化させ続ける。そうした視点やしくみづくりが、こどもの空間をつくるにあたって、大切な思想になると感じた。

（松本麻里）

Nishida : The Ministry of Land, Infrastructure, Transport and Tourism's standards for park playground equipment were reexamined in 2008 and 2014, and their safety has been improving. However, measures at schools and commercial facilities are still not sufficient. I think this is a problem that we should work on going forward.

—— Is there anything you want to try in the future?

Nishida : AI-based protective systems have reached a very high level, so I think that new methods could be developed to prevent untouched accidents that occur in everyday life, such as falling from balconies and drowning in bathtubs. All parents have moments when they take their eyes of off their children, so I think that it would be ideal to go in the direction of installing cameras and sensors, and protecting children using a combination of human protection and AI, rather than just the human eye. It would be great if this could be done at customer-attracting facilities and parks as well.

Yamanaka : The Japan Pediatric Society's website has an "Injury Alert" section where cases are posted that we as pediatricians have experienced on site. Anyone can view this section. It is extremely easy to understand and has led to the revision of various standards, so I would like for it to be expanded. This is currently only being done in pediatrics, but I think that if other fields got involved and the entire medical care industry recorded and shared data, hundreds of cases would be gathered every day. I think they need to be analyzed with AI and made into a database that would be useful in preventing accidents.

About three years ago, we launched an NPO, Safe Kids Japan, and began activities to educate and enlighten guardians. There is a definite trend to accidents that children are likely to incur at each month of age, so it is easy to provide information ahead of time. For example, accidental swallowing is sure to occur once a child turns 6 months old, and, in this age of advanced communication methods, it would most likely be possible to create a system where alerts are received via smartphone during that period. I want to continue with effective enlightenment activities.

Summary

There is a limit to how many children's accidents can be prevented with only the human eye. Preventing accidents requires creativity in spatial creation and the incorporation of technology. Spatial design in particular must consider the safety of a variety of people, rather than simply pursuing an aesthetic outlook. Even after a space is completed, it is necessary to understand how it is used and constantly make improvements and changes to the space and how it is managed. I felt the importance of having these perspectives and schemes when creating spaces for children. (Mari Matsumoto)

▌概要 **Summary**

NPO 法人 **Safe Kids Japan** ／ NPO Safe Kids Japan
http://safekidsjapan.org/
国立研究開発法人産業技術総合研究所 臨界副都心センター／
National Institute of Advanced Industrial Science and Technology, Tokyo Waterfront
http://www.aist.go.jp/waterfront/

3 空間デザイン
Spatial design

こどもの空間をデザインする際に検討すべき項目として、スケール、色彩、明るさ／照明、素材、アイテムなどについて基本的な考え方を示した。もちろん、正解はひとつではない。ここに示す考え方を参考として、それぞれのデザインの現場で検討してもらいたい。

A basic concept was presented using scale, color, brightness/lighting, materials, objects, etc. as items that should be considered when designing children's spaces. Of course, there is no one correct way. Use these concepts as a reference when considering the site for each design.

スケール
Scale

ひとりになりたいとき、親子で過ごしたいとき、大勢で体験を共有したいときなど、それぞれの活動に適切な広さを確保する。併せて、こどもの身体寸法を理解して、ふさわしいスケールで設計することが基本となる。

Ensure the appropriate amount of space for each activity, whether people want to be alone, spend time with their children, or share an experience with a crowd. At the same time, the basic rule is to know the body measurements of children and design using an appropriate scale.

色彩
Color

こどもっぽい色彩計画（「女の子はピンクを好む」というような先入観にもとづくもの）を安易に採用しない。また、こどもだけでなく、ともに利用する親をはじめとする大人にも配慮する。

Do not automatically go for a childish color scheme (one based on a preconception such as "girls like pink").
In addition, consider not only children, but also adults such as the ones that will be using the space with their children.

明るさ／照明
Brightness/lighting

こどもの多様な活動（静かな読書、活発な運動など）に応じた適切な明るさを確保する。明るいことが必ずしも適切でない場合があることに留意する。

Ensure appropriate lighting for various children's activities (quiet reading, active exercise, etc.).
Consider that a bright place is not always the appropriate choice.

> するとそこには大きな岩がありました…
> And then, there was a big rock...

> いいぞ〜！ かんばれ〜！
> Good job!
> Keep going!

素材
Materials

舐めても人体に悪影響がない素材を採用
する。同時に、舐めたあとの清掃のしやすさ
にも配慮する。また、転びにくい、滑りにくい
素材を採用するとともに、つまずいたり、落
ちたりしても、大けがにつながらない素材
や工法を検討する。

Use materials that will not have a negative effect
on the human body if they are licked. At the same
time, consider the ease of cleaning licked surfaces.
In addition, use materials that are hard to trip over
or slip on, and consider materials and construction
methods that will not lead to major injuries if
children trip or fall.

あーむ
Yum!

!

なるほど！
Oh, I see!

アイテムなど
Objects, etc.

受動的になりがちな情報機器ばか
りではなく、自らの働きかけで変化
を生み出すアイテムも検討する。た
とえば、つまみを回すとパーツが動
くアートワーク、ボタン操作による
参加型の展示なども有効だろう。

Rather than using only information
devices, which tend to be passive, consider
objects that will generate changes with
independent movements. For example, a
piece of art where the parts move when
a lever is turned or a hands-on button-
operated exhibit are sure to be effective.

まわってる！
It's turning!

なんだろう？
What's this?

うごいた！
It moved!

こどもの身体データ

Appendix: Children's Physicalt Data

監修:NPO法人Safe Kids Japan 理事長 山中龍宏／国立研究開発法人 産業技術総合研究所 西田佳史
参考文献:『子どものからだ図鑑 キッズデザイン実践のためのデータブック』
企画・監修: 独立行政法人 産業技術総合研究所 デジタルヒューマン工学研究センター／公益社団法人 日本インダストリアルデザイナー協会／特定非営利活動法人(内閣府認証NPO) キッズデザイン協議会

Supervisors:Tatsuhiro Yamanaka, Chief Director, Safe Kids Japan (NPO) , Yoshifumi Nishida, National Institute of Advanced Industrial Science and Technology (AIST)
References:An Illustrated Guide to a Child's Body: A Data Book for Practicing Kid's Design
Planning /Supervision: National Institute of Advanced Industrial Science and Technology (AIST) , Digital Human Research Center, Japan Industrial Designers' Association (JIDA), Kids Design Association (Cabinet Office-approved NPO)

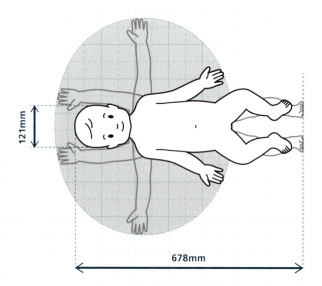

121mm

678mm

100mm

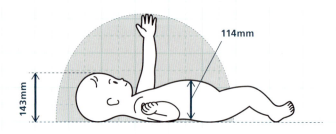

143mm

114mm

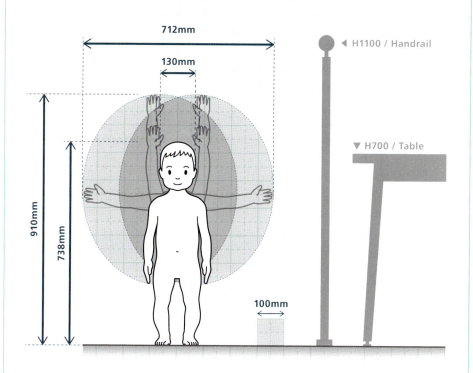

712mm
130mm
910mm
738mm
100mm
◀ H1100 / Handrail
▼ H700 / Table

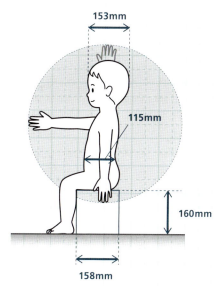

153mm
115mm
160mm
158mm

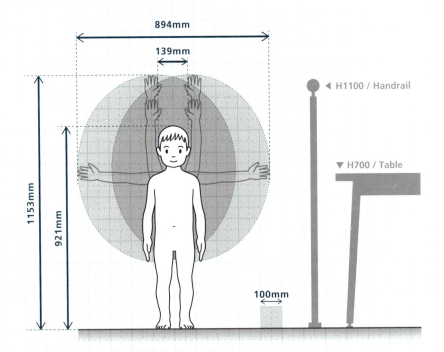

894mm
139mm
1153mm
921mm
◀ H1100 / Handrail
▼ H700 / Table
100mm

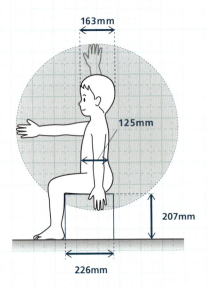

163mm
125mm
207mm
226mm

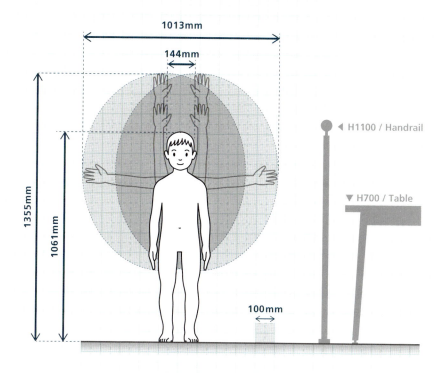

1013mm

144mm

1355mm

1061mm

◀ H1100 / Handrail

▼ H700 / Table

100mm

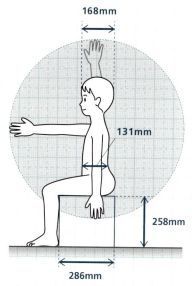

168mm

131mm

258mm

286mm

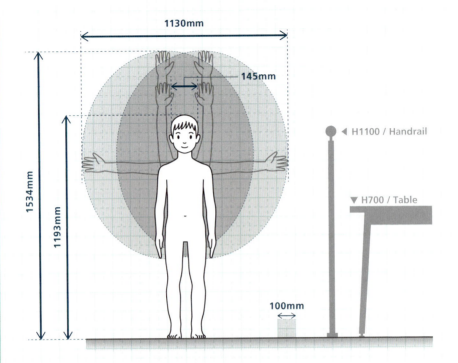

1130mm

145mm

1534mm

1193mm

◀ H1100 / Handrail

▼ H700 / Table

100mm

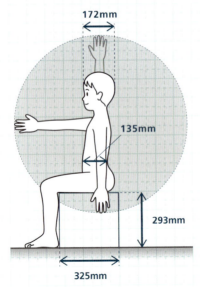

172mm

135mm

293mm

325mm

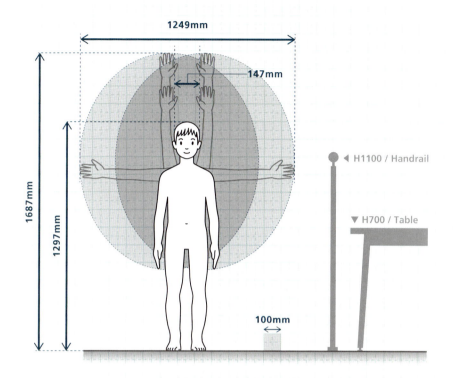

1249mm

147mm

1687mm

1297mm

H1100 / Handrail

H700 / Table

100mm

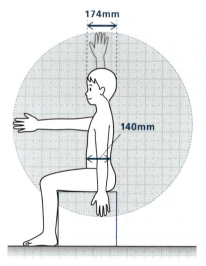

174mm

140mm

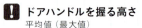 **ドアハンドルを握る高さ** Height at which a child can grab a door handle
平均値（最大値） Average value（maximum value）

200mm

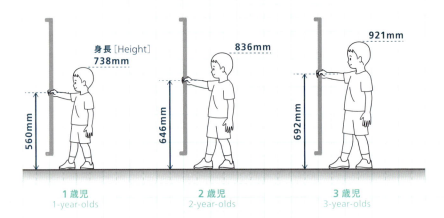

身長 [Height]
738mm
560mm

1 歳児
1-year-olds

836mm
646mm

2 歳児
2-year-olds

921mm
692mm

3 歳児
3-year-olds

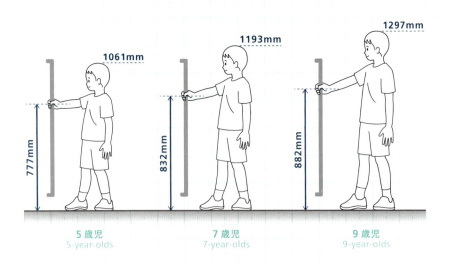

1061mm
777mm

5 歳児
5-year-olds

1193mm
832mm

7 歳児
7-year-olds

1297mm
882mm

9 歳児
9-year-olds

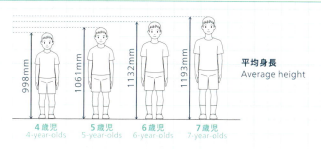

平均身長
Average height

4 歳児 4-year-olds 998mm
5 歳児 5-year-olds 1061mm
6 歳児 6-year-olds 1132mm
7 歳児 7-year-olds 1193mm

⚠ 乗り越えられる高さ　Height at which a child can grab a door handle
平均値（最大値）　Average value（maximum value）

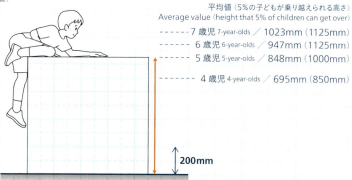

平均値（5%の子どもが乗り越えられる高さ）
Average value（height that 5% of children can get over）

- - - - - - 7 歳児 7-year-olds ／ 1023mm（1125mm）
- - - - - - 6 歳児 6-year-olds ／ 947mm（1125mm）
- - - - - - 5 歳児 5-year-olds ／ 848mm（1000mm）
- - - - - - 4 歳児 4-year-olds ／ 695mm（850mm）

200mm

⚠ すり抜けられる幅　Width children can get through　Average value（minimum value）
平均値（最小値）

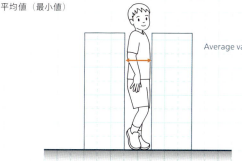

平均値（5%の子どもが乗り越えられる高さ）
Average value（width that 5% of children can get through）

7 歳児 7-year-olds ／ 129mm（110mm）
6 歳児 6-year-olds ／ 128mm（110mm）
5 歳児 5-year-olds ／ 119mm（100mm）
4 歳児 4-year-olds ／ 115mm（100mm）

⚠ くぐり抜けられる高さ　Height children can get under　Average value（minimum value）
平均値（最小値）

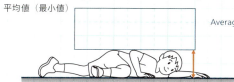

平均値（5%の子どもがくぐり抜けられる高さ）
Average value（height that 5% of children can get under）

7 歳児 7-year-olds ／ 150mm（140mm）
6 歳児 6-year-olds ／ 150mm（140mm）
5 歳児 5-year-olds ／ 147mm（140mm）
4 歳児 4-year-olds ／ 145mm（130mm）

※イラストは 5 歳児をもとに作成しています。0～3 歳は実験指示が難しく、今回は 4 歳以上を対象としました。
※ The illustrations are based on a 5-year-old. As it is difficult to give experiment instructions to children
　3 years old and younger, this study targeted children of 4 years and older.

おわりに

　こどもも大人も居心地がよい空間とは、どんな空間だろう。

　取材を終えて思うのは、こどもも大人も自分の居場所があって、そこを訪れる人、働く人、すべての人が安心して快適な時間を過ごせるところ。どんな人でもあたりまえに同じ空間で過ごし、交流し、お互いを認め合えるしくみとデザインが重要であり、必要だということがわかりました。

　一人ひとりが、のびのびと心を解き放ち、充実した、心に残る経験ができる場所…そう考えたとき、日々空間づくりにかかわる私たちは、居場所が本当に必要な人びとに、居心地のよい空間を届けられているだろうか？

　思いっきりあそべる場所やほっとする居場所がなくて、未来を描けなくなっているこどもたちもいる。そんなこどもたちが、自分を肯定できる経験や「ようこそ」ともてなされている感覚、実感をもてる。そうした場としくみづくりに向き合う、その手段として空間のデザインを活かしていきたいという思いをより一層強くもつようになりました。

　すべての人びとへ「ようこそ」の気持ちを込めた空間を届ける。それに向かって挑戦する取り組みを続けていきます。

　今回のインタビューでは、自分も一人の実践者として、出会った方たちの言葉に背中を押され、たくさんの勇気をもらいました。惜しみなく施設にかける思いや場づくりのプロセスを話してくださったことに、この場を借りて心から感謝します。そして、この本を手に取ってくださった読者の方へも心より感謝の意を表します。ありがとうございました。

松本麻里

Conclusion

So what makes "a space that is comfortable for both children and adults?"

After completing our work, we believe the definition to be a place where children and adults both belong, and one in which the people who visit it, work in it, and everyone else is able to spend a safe and relaxing time. We learned the importance and necessity of schemes and designs that allow anyone to naturally spend time, interact, and recognize one another within the same place.

A place where each person can open their hearts wide and have a fulfilling, memorable experience...when thinking of such a place, have we, as persons involved in spatial creation every day, been successful in delivering comfortable spaces to those who truly need somewhere to belong?

Some children have no place in which they can play to their hearts' content or relax, making it impossible for them to imagine their futures. These children need places where they can experience self-affirmation and feel welcome. We now have an even stronger desire to meet the challenge of creating such places and systems using spatial design as a method to do so.

Delivering spaces where everyone feels welcome — we will continue our efforts to work toward that challenge.

As a practitioner myself, I gained support and encouragement from the words of the people that I met during the interviews. I would like to use this opportunity to express my heartfelt appreciation to those interviewees for freely discussing the thought put into facilities and the spatial creation process.

I would also like to express my deep gratitude to the readers who picked up this book. Thank you very much

Mari Matsumoto

謝辞

　本書の出版にあたっては、多くの方々にご尽力いただきました。まず、インタビュー調査にご協力いただいた方々に改めてお礼を申し上げます。こどもと関わる現場から生み出される言葉には、いつも蒙を啓かれる思いでした。紙面の都合上、すべてを掲載できませんでしたが、こどもも大人も心地よく過ごす空間という視点から共有すべきメッセージをのがさず読者に届けるよう心がけました。

　一方で、言うまでもなく、インタビュー先の宣伝や提灯持ちのような原稿は一切書かないということを大前提として定めていました。本書に記載された内容は、あくまでも複数の調査にもとづき客観的に情報を抽出したうえで執筆したものです。

　また、本書は日英併記としています。これは、日本におけることも環境に対する取り組みを広く世界に伝えるべきと考えたためです。とかく「海外の事例はすばらしく、それにひきかえ日本は」という論調になりがちな風潮がみられますが、こども環境についていえば、世界に誇るべき点は多々あります。これを伝えたいと考えました。翻訳にあたってはTransPerfect さんにお世話になりました。的確な翻訳に感謝します。同時に、日本における取り組みは特殊なものではなく、諸外国でも同様の考えにもとづく取り組みがあることを示すため、シンガポールとスウェーデンの事例を取り上げました。海外調査の一部をコーディネートしてくれたYan Yan Cao さんの尽力に感謝します。

　本書の装丁はマツダオフィスの松田行正さんと梶原結実さんにお願いしました。こどもに迎合するようなこどもだましの姿勢ではなく、専門性を

Acknowledgements

Many people contributed to the publication of this book. First of all, we would like to once again thank everyone who cooperated in the interviews. It felt like we were constantly being enlightened by the words generated at each of these sites involved with children. Though there is not enough space to mention everyone, we have done our best to provide readers with the full message through the lens of spaces that are comfortable for both children and adults. However, needless to say, we had established as a fundamental premise that we would not advertise or praise the interviewees or their facilities in any way in the manuscript. This book is composed of information that was objectively extracted from multiple studies.

In addition, it is written in both Japanese and English. This is because we believed that the world should be aware of our efforts in Japan regarding environments for children. Discussions tend to claim that "overseas cases are great, but Japan's are inferior"; however, when speaking of children's environments, there are many world-class achievements that we should be proud of. We wanted to express this. The English translation was done by TransPerfect Japan G.K. We thank them for the precise translation. At the same time, we also included cases from Singapore and Sweden in order to show that many of the efforts being made in Japan are not unique, but based on the same concepts as certain foreign countries. We are also grateful for the efforts of Yan Yan Cao, who coordinated some of the overseas studies.

This book was bound by Yukimasa Matsuda and Yumi Kajiwara of MATZDA OFFICE. We believe that, rather than adopting the attitude of pandering to children, using expertise to implement efforts that aim to provide true experiences will result in a space that is comfortable for both children and adults. We truly appreciate them for providing graphic design that fits perfectly

もって本物を志向して取り組むことによって、こどもにも大人にも心地よい空間デザインが生まれる。このようなわたしたちの考え方にぴったり合ったグラフィックデザインを提示してくれたことに敬意を表します。また、第3章のイラストレーションは成田治子さんにお願いしました。こどもたちの生き生きとした表情や細やかなしぐさは、ご自身が子育て中だからこそ描けるものでしょう。共感とともに謝意を表します。

「こどもあるある」などのアイデアは、東洋大学ライフデザイン学部人間環境デザイン学科の学生たちによるところが大きく、その瑞々しい視点は笑いを誘う共通体験を思い起こさせてくれました。次世代を担う学生たちにとっても本書が貢献するところがあれば、うれしく思います。

　そして、錯綜する膨大な情報を整理し、常に冷静に指摘してくれた産学社の末澤寧史さんに感謝します。なにげない問いかけを含め、末澤さんのあらゆる言葉は、わたしたちの視野を広げ、考えを深めるきっかけとなりました。本を書くということがこんなにもおもしろい仕事だと実感できたのは、末澤さんのおかげです。

　最後に、いつも支えてくれる家族に感謝します。「はじめに」(p.002)で述べたように、わたしたちはみな母親で、仕事をしながら子育てをしています。ときに、どちらもうまくいかずに悩むこともありますが、こどもたちとの日々の暮らしがあるからこそ本書は生まれました。ともにいてくれて、ありがとう。

2018年1月

仲 綾子 ＋ TeamM 乃村工藝社

※本書における調査の一部は、JSPS科研費JP16K06665の助成を受けたものです。

with this concept. The illustrations in Chapter 3 were drawn by Haruko Narita. Her ability to bring children's lively expressions and detailed gestures to life is no doubt due to the fact that she is currently raising children herself. We express our understanding as well as our gratitude.

The ideas for sections such as "Common occurrences with children" came largely from the students of the Department of Human Environment Design, Faculty of Human Life Design at Toyo University. Their fresh perspectives brought back memories of common experiences that made us laugh. We hope that this book is helpful to the students who shoulder the next generation.

We would also like to thank Yasufumi Suezawa of Sangakusha Co., Ltd., who organized a vast amount of intricate information and always pointed it out to us calmly. All of Mr. Suezawa's words, including his casual inquiries, gave us an opportunity to widen our field of view and deepen our thoughts. It is thanks to Mr. Suezawa that we were able to experience how interesting the job of writing a book can be.

Lastly, we would like to thank our families who always support us. As noted in the Introduction (p.002), we are all mothers who are working while raising children. There are times when neither of these go right and we become distressed, but it was our daily lives spent with our children that made this book possible. Thank you for being here with us.

January 2018
Ayako Naka + TeamM Produced by NOMURA Co., Ltd.

※Some of the studies included in this book were funded
by JSPS's Grants-in-Aid for Scientific Research (KAKENHI) JP16K06665.

Profiles

仲 綾子（なか あやこ）

東洋大学 ライフデザイン学部 人間環境デザイン学科 准教授。博士(工学)
京都大学卒業、東京工業大学大学院修了。環境デザイン研究所、厚生労
働省を経て現職。専門はこども環境、医療福祉建築。国土交通省「女性
が輝く社会づくりにつながるトイレ等の環境整備・利用のあり方に関す
る協議会」構成員（2015）、経済産業省「商業施設内の遊戯施設における
消費者安全に関する検討会」座長（2016）、日本建築学会 子ども教育支
援会議 子ども教育事業部会 部会長（2017）ほか。主著に、日本建築学会編：
「楽々建築・楽々都市−"すまい・まち・地球"自分との関係を見つけるワー
クショップ」、技報堂出版、2011（共著）ほか。主な設計に、こども病院、
小学校、保育園、ベビー休憩室、住宅ほか。

[執筆箇所：はじめに、第1章、第2章（事例1-2,3-2,4-1,4-2,4-3、コラム2,3、トピッ
クス）、第3章]

TeamM 乃村工藝社（チームエム のむらこうげいしゃ）

乃村工藝社は人びとに感動を提供する「空間」をつくり、活性化する企業。
同社の育休明け社員で構成された「TeamM（チームM）」は「未来の子
どもたちのための場と仕組みをつくる」をコンセプトに2015年に発足。
空間づくりと育児の経験を活かした企画デザインの提案、産学連携の調
査研究などさまざまな活動を行っている。

・松本 麻里（まつもと まり）

武蔵野美術大学卒業後、1991年乃村工藝社入社。入社以来ミュージア
ムの展示デザインに携り、TeamM発足時より従事。空間のジャンルを
問わず安心安全快適なこどもと過ごす空間づくりのプランニング、デ
ザイン、ワークショップ、ファシリテーションを実践している。社外活
動では美術館を拠点に美術鑑賞ファシリテーション、アートイベント企
画実施などを行っている。

[執筆箇所：第2章（事例2-2,2-3,コラム1,4）、第3章、おわりに]

・井部 玲子（いべ れいこ）

武蔵工業大学（現・東京都市大学）卒業、2005年乃村工藝社入社。空間を
通じてコミュニケーションを創出するさまざまな分野での開発・プロ
ジェクト推進業務を担当。主にオフィス環境や企業PR施設、展示会、
各種イベントなどの空間づくりに従事。TeamMでは、こどもに関わる
空間づくりの調査やツール作成、プランニングに携わる。

[執筆箇所：第2章（事例2-1,3-1,3-3）]

・西本 彩（にしもと あや）

早稲田大学卒業後、2002年乃村工藝社入社。入社以来、ショッピング
センター、各種専門店など、商業分野を中心としたプロジェクト推進や
開発事業を担当。現在は「子育てが楽しくできる環境を場づくりから」
をテーマに、さまざまな事業企画を進める。

[執筆箇所：第2章（事例1-1,1-3、トピックス）]

Ayako Naka

Associate Professor, Department of Human Environment Design, Faculty of Human Life Design, Toyo University. Doctor of Engineering

Naka graduated from Kyoto University and completed her graduate degree at Tokyo Institute of Technology. She has previously worked at the Environment Design Institute and the Ministry of Health, Labour, and Welfare. She specializes in designing children's environments and medical and welfare architecture. She was, among others, a member of the Ministry of Land, Infrastructure, Transport, and Tourism's "Council on the Environmental Maintenance and Use of Restrooms, etc. Leading to the Building of a Society where Women Shine," (2015) ; chairperson of the Ministry of Economy, Trade, and Industry's "Study Group for Consumer Safety in Play Facilities on the Premises of Commercial Facilities" (2016) ; chairperson of the Architectural Institute of Japan's Committee to Support Children's Education, Children's Education Activities Subcommittee (2017) . Major works include "Rakuraku (enjoy/easy) Architecture, Rakuraku (enjoy/easy) City: 'Your House, Your Town, and the Earth'—A Workshop to Discover How They Relate to You," Architectural Institute of Japan (co-author) , Gihodo Shuppan, 2011. Major designs include children's hospitals, elementary schools, nursery schools, baby rooms, houses, etc.

Portions authored: Introduction, Chapter 1, Chapter 2 (Cases 1-2, 3-2, 4-1, 4-2, and 4-3, Columns 2 and 3, Topics) , Chapter 3

TeamM Produced by NOMURA Co., Ltd.

NOMURA is a company that creates and invigorates "spaces" that inspire people. Touting the concept of "building spaces and schemes for children in the future," the company's "Team M" conducts a variety of activities such as planning, design proposals, industry-academia collaborative research studies, using their experience in spatial creation and child-raising.

・Mari Matsumoto

After graduating from Musashino Art University, she joined NOMURA Co., Ltd. in 1991. Since joining the company, she has been involved in designing exhibits for museums and has been a member of Team M since its inception. She has been involved in the planning, design, workshop, and facilitation aspects of the creation of a variety of spaces in which people can spend time with children safely, securely, and comfortably. Her overseas activities include various work with art museums such as the facilitation of art appreciation as well the planning and implementation of art events.

Portions authored: Chapter 2 (Cases 2-2 and 2-3, Columns 1 and 4) , Chapter 3, Conclusion

・Reiko Ibe

After graduating from the Musashi Institute of Technology (now Tokyo City University) , she joined NOMURA Co., Ltd. in 2005. She has handled development and project promotion duties in various fields that use space to create opportunities for communication. She is mainly involved in creating spaces such as office environments, corporate PR facilities, and various events. At Team M, she is involved in studies, tool creation, and planning for the creation of spaces relating to children.

Portions authored: Chapter 2 (Cases 2-1, 3-1, and 3-3)

・Aya Nishimoto

After graduating from Waseda University, she joined NOMURA Co., Ltd. in 2002. Since joining the company, she has handled project promotion and the development business with a focus on the commercial field, such as shopping centers and various specialty stores. She currently promotes various business projects under the theme of "using spatial creation to build environments where raising children is fun."

Portions authored: Chapter 2 (Cases 1-1 and 1-3, Topics)

ブックデザイン：松田行正＋梶原結実（マツダオフィス）
イラスト（Chapter3）：成田治子
企画協力：小島敏明
執筆協力：吉田真緒
調査協力：小林優里、佐藤沙樹
海外調査協力：Yan Yan Cao
翻訳：トランスパーフェクト・ジャパン
編集担当：末澤寧史

Book design: Yukimasa Matsuda, Yumi Kajiwara (MATZDAOFFICE)
Illustrations (Chapter 3) : Haruko Narita
Planning assistance: Toshiaki Kojima
Writing assistance: Mao Yoshida
Study assistance: Yuri Kobayashi, Saki Sato
Overseas study assistance: Yan Yan Cao
Translation: TransPerfect Japan G.K.
Editor: Yasufumi Suezawa

こどもとおとなの空間デザイン ［対訳］

初版 1 刷発行 ● 2018年 1月31日

編著者

仲 綾子＋TeamM 乃村工藝社

発行者

薗部良徳

発行所

（株）産学社

〒101-0061 東京都千代田区神田三崎町2-20-7 水道橋西口会館　Tel. 03（6272）9313　Fax. 03（3515）3660
http://sangakusha.jp/

印刷所

（株）ティーケー出版印刷

©Ayako Naka+TeamM Produced by NOMURA Co., Ltd. 2018, Printed in Japan
ISBN: 978-4-7825-3467-0 C3052